D0405523

# The Soulful Art *of* Persuasion

"There are books that help you in your profession and there are books that help you become a better person. *The Soulful Art of Persuasion* will help you get better in your profession as a side effect of becoming a better person. That's the beauty of this book."

—Aubrey Marcus, founder and CEO of Onnit; *New York Times* bestselling author of *Own the Day, Own Your Life*

"The habits and engaging storytelling in these pages provide a perfect framework for anyone who wants to build meaningful relationships in all facets of life from the personal to the political."

—Zeppa Kreager, chief of staff for The Biden for President campaign

"Jason Harris is a Jedi in the art of using soulful persuasion to put some good into the world. This book is required reading for anyone who wants to be a Purpose-driven leader."

—Afdhel Aziz, founder and Chief Purpose Officer of Conspiracy of Love; coauthor of *Good Is the New Cool: Market Like You Give a Damn*

"As our world drowns in tweets, posts, and 24-hour news cycles, the art of persuasion has never been harder, yet more important. Fortunately, Jason Harris has given us the playbook to build the character, empathy, and engagement needed to skillfully win over others in this new media world of distrust."

—Eric Ryan, cofounder of Method and Olly

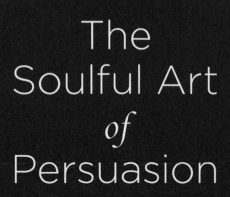

# The
# Soulful Art
# *of*
# Persuasion

### THE 11 HABITS
### THAT WILL MAKE ANYONE
### A MASTER INFLUENCER

# JASON HARRIS

CURRENCY
NEW YORK

CURRENCY and its colophon are trademarks
of Penguin Random House LLC.

Currency books are available at special discounts for
bulk purchases for sales promotions or corporate use.
Special editions, including personalized covers, excerpts
of existing books, or books with corporate logos, can be
created in large quantities for special needs. For more
information, contact Premium Sales at (212) 572-2232 or
e-mail specialmarkets@penguinrandomhouse.com.

Library of Congress Cataloging-in-Publication Data
Names: Harris, Jason (Economist) author.
Title: The soulful art of persuasion: the 11 habits that will make anyone
    a master influencer / Jason Harris.
Description: 1 Edition. | New York: Currency, 2019. | Includes
    bibliographical references and index.
Identifiers: LCCN 2019003576 | ISBN 9781984822567 (hardback)
Subjects: LCSH: Success in business. | Persuasion (Psychology) |
    Marketing—Psychological aspects. | Communication in marketing. |
    BISAC: BUSINESS & ECONOMICS / Negotiating. | BUSINESS &
    ECONOMICS / Marketing / Research.
Classification: LCC HF5386 .H2734 2019 | DDC 658.4/09019—dc23
    LC record available at https://lccn.loc.gov/2019003576

ISBN 978-1-9848-2256-7
Ebook ISBN 978-1-9848-2257-4
International Edition ISBN 978-0-593-13607-2

Printed in the United States of America

Book design by Andrea Lau
Illustrations by Stefanie Gomez

10 9 8 7 6 5 4 3 2 1

First Edition

*To all those on the journey of soulful success*

# Contents

# PRINCIPLE 3: **EMPATHETIC** ⊘

# PRINCIPLE 4: **SOULFUL** ⚠

The Soulful Art *of* Persuasion

# The Starting Point

It's hard to know who to trust anymore.

These days you can't look at a screen without being hit in the face with phony outrage, fake news, phishing scams, pop-up ads, or some other kind of online stupidity. Trust in government and mainstream media is near historical lows.[1] And if anybody ever blindly trusted Silicon Valley giants like Facebook and Google, they don't anymore.[2] Most Americans don't even trust opinion polls—according to one opinion poll, at least.[3]

So, how do you persuade people in an environment where nobody has a reason to trust you—where people are actively looking for reasons to be suspicious? That's the challenge I've spent my career grappling with. Because this much is clear: Americans sure as hell don't trust people in my line of work.

As the CEO of the creative advertising agency Mekanism, I belong to one of the least-trusted professions in the world. The only people considered more dishonest, according to a Gallup survey, are used-car salesmen and members of Congress.[4] That's some pretty questionable company.

These attitudes say a lot about the nature of influence in the modern era. Because if there's one thing all three of these professions have in common, it's that each is in the business of persuasion. And when you picture someone who persuades for a living, two types of people spring to mind.

One is a slippery, fast-talking operator trying to pull one over on us, like the desperate real estate brokers in the Pulitzer Prize–winning play *Glengarry Glen Ross*. These are the sorts of characters who will tell you anything you want to hear, just to close a deal. They rely on vague promises, linguistic tricks, and fine print to hide the truth. They annoyingly keep repeating your name as if they know you. They are purposely inoffensive, way too self-aware, calculating, eager to please, and, in a word, *soulless*. Nobody wants to buy anything from these people; they make us want to figure out any excuse to say no.

At the other extreme are ideologues and loudmouths who are absolutely certain of their point of view and think anyone who disagrees with them is either stupid or dangerous. Think cable-news partisans and Internet trolls, Washington lobbyists and talk-radio pseudo-intellectuals. People in this group can be found at all points on our political spectrum. And they are incapable of convincing anybody who hasn't already embraced their exact same worldview.

As a leading practitioner in the advertising industry, I find myself up against these preconceptions daily. Yet I've still managed to build a career around my ability to persuade—whether I'm helping persuade consumers to buy certain products and services, persuading clients to hire our agency and to remain with us, persuading potential employees to come on board, or persuading our current employees to do their best work. I've managed to do this in an industry in which persuasion happens in the most scrutinized environment imaginable.

What's my secret? Well, I've only found one solution that works in today's modern world: be the opposite of the greasy salesperson or the self-deluded blowhard everyone is on guard against. Be someone people can trust and relate to and even sometimes be moved by.

In other words, you have to be *soulful*.

That's the driving idea behind *The Soulful Art of Persuasion*. And it's based on the simple observation that whether someone persuades us or not has little to do with the exact words and phrases they use or the positions they take, but with the kind of person they really are.

Persuasive people aren't skilled at sweet-talking their audience or figuring out what people want to hear. Rather, they are the individuals we want to agree with. They have qualities that compel us to be on their side and trust them, whatever the issue may be. Their persuasiveness comes from their *soul*.

The result is a form of influence that is far more powerful than reason alone. Logical arguments *force* us to accept a certain conclusion whether we like it or not, but soulful persuasion *attracts* us to a position. Genuine persuasion is about *engaging* rather than *insisting*. And this can actually be learned and made habitual with practice.

I'm not going to give you a collection of tricks for closing a deal or making a quick sale. What I *will* show you is how to develop the personal habits that will allow you to be the kind of person that others trust, seek advice from, and want to collaborate with.

In short, I'll show you how to develop a more persuasive *character.*

Character is the collection of traits, dispositions, and virtues that someone consistently displays in their thoughts, emotional responses, and actions—the qualities that reflect who we are. Developing a persuasive character means acquiring the character traits, habits of mind, and personal practices that, once truly internalized, will no doubt make you a more influential person.

## The Four Principles

Personal dispositions that can make you persuasive fall into four main categories.

First, persuasive people are *original.* When they speak, you sense they are coming from a place of authenticity and honesty and that you're getting a glimpse of the real, unique them—not some prepackaged version designed to please you. For people who possess this virtue, their thoughts and actions are motivated by a deep understanding of who they are, always being themselves and building deep, long-term commitments; they are not motivated by the desire for short-term gains.

Second, persuasive people are *generous.* They give habitually and without expecting things in return. I'm not just talking about money or physical gifts. Persuasive people also are generous with advice, opportunities, introductions, respect, and emotional positivity. You never get the impression that they are just looking out for themselves.

Third, persuasive people are *empathetic.* They are naturally curious about other people and seek out engaging conversations that delve past small talk into topics that genuinely matter to others. People of this sort are skilled collaborators and possess an outlook that emphasizes our common humanity, not our differences.

Finally, persuasive people are *soulful*. They hold themselves to their own self-imposed ethical and personal standards, always strive to be better, and motivate others to push beyond their normal limits. They are sources of inspiration for those around them. As a result, they possess a personal authority that makes them naturally influential.

I'll explore these four principles in detail while focusing on the eleven specific habits that fall out of these larger principles, how they contribute to persuasion, and what each of us can do to develop and strengthen them.

My goal is to help you incorporate certain attributes, viewpoints, and tendencies into your way of life, so that they become reflexive, habitual, and a part of who you are. This way, when you display empathy or generosity or soulfulness, it will be obvious to those around you that they are getting a glimpse of your character—even if that recognition is unconscious.

Depending on your own natural strengths and weaknesses, some of the following chapters will be more useful than others. Readers who are naturally empathetic, for example, don't need to spend too much time strengthening that aspect of their character.

The best way to use this book is to be honest with yourself about which traits need the most work, and focus on those practices that will do the most good for you.

## Making Persuasion Soulful Again

"Persuasion" isn't exactly a heartwarming word. It is kind of loaded, and most people associate it with deception or some form of coercion. There's no doubt that negative persuasion is possible. In fact, you see it everywhere in the form of fear-mongering, political attack ads, and "us versus them" rhetoric. And my own industry, advertising, certainly bears some responsibility for persuasion's bad rap.

But persuasion can also come from a positive, life-affirming place—a *soulful* place.

If you strive to be original, generous, empathetic, and soulful, you will be well on your way to a more rewarding and meaningful life. You will also be a happier, more positive person with more fulfilling experiences.

That these character traits will also make you more influential in a wide range of situations is largely a side benefit. But that doesn't change the fact that these principles are profoundly relevant for anyone hoping to become more influential—at home, at work, among friends, or even in the wider world.

When people are won over by your character, they are usually motivated by their own best tendencies. These include their recognition of our common humanity, their willingness to see things from a different point of view, their sense of possibility, and their desire to act on positive emotions.

The current culture of political polarization, online echo chambers, and tribalism is one in which persuasion is sorely lacking. For us to move past our differences and find a way to live better together, we're all going to need to become better at persuading each other.

At the same time, character matters a lot more than it used to. Thanks to the cultural shifts of the last few years, forms of discrimination, misogyny, and racism that once were swept under the rug are now being called out. A person's deficits of character can prove career-ending. This is all the more reason to approach persuasion from a standpoint that puts character front and center.

*The Soulful Art of Persuasion* is for entrepreneurs, wannapreneurs, executives, creative types, and anyone who wants to utilize the power of persuasion to bring colleagues, peers, clients, friends, or loved ones to their point of view. After all, at some level, all of us are in the business of persuading.

Of course, you can't fake being a persuasive person, any more than you can fake being a great classical pianist, free-throw shooter, or neurosurgeon. But anyone can learn to be one. I've had to learn to be one over the course of more than two decades in the cutthroat business of advertising.

What you hold in your hands will help you do the same.

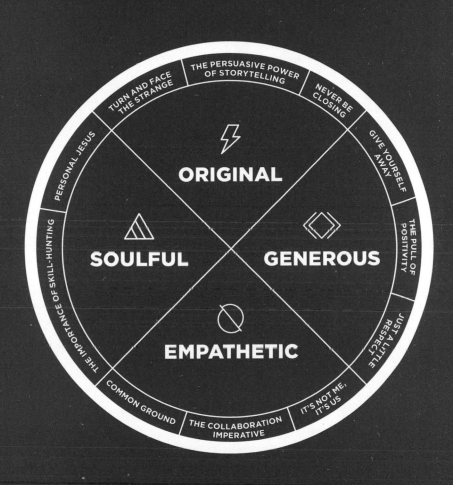

# PRINCIPLE 1

# ORIGINAL

When a person is truly persuasive, we never doubt that what
they're saying comes from someplace real. Even if we disagree
with them, we still recognize
that they stand for something
and that they aren't afraid to
show us who they are and what
they value.
These are the kinds of people who care more about being
true to themselves than about
just getting to a yes, convincing
others how great they are, im-
pressing the boss, closing a few
extra sales, or besting someone in an argument. That's why
being your most original, genuine self is such an essential component of persuasiveness.
By definition, being yourself can't
be faked. If you present your true self, people will be far
more willing to hear you out,
take you at your word, and
side with you on conten-
tious issues.
When        someone
is    unapologetically
original,    we    can
feel   in   our   gut
that    they    are
worthy of our
loyalty,    our
allegiance,
and,   yes,
o      u      r
b u s i -
ness.

Chapter 1

# turn and face the strange

---

*So I turned myself to face me*
*But I've never caught a glimpse*
*How the others must see the faker*
*I'm much too fast to take that test*

—David Bowie, "Changes"

My idol has always been David Bowie. Nobody has ever been better at following the advice often attributed to Oscar Wilde: "Be yourself, everybody else is already taken." Over five decades in the music, fashion, and entertainment industries, Bowie never stopped exploring who he was and finding new ways to inspire others with his gender-bending, music-blending creativity. Most of all, as a role model, he made it all right for me and many others to be our own weird and wonderful selves. He made anyone and everyone comfortable to fly their unique freak flag.

Growing up as a child of the 1980s, I caught the second and

third waves of Bowie's work. "Let's Dance," "China Girl," and "Under Pressure" were the first hits that made me take notice: "Let's sway / While color lights up your face / Let's sway / Sway through the crowd to an empty space." Bowie swayed me. He convinced me because he was one of a kind. He persuaded me with his stories. And from there I was off with all-night sojourns into the entire Bowie canon. His albums mixed an astonishing array of genres, from art rock to glam rock to post-punk, electronica, hard rock, jazz, new wave, and unfortunately even disco. There was nothing he couldn't do.

I'm not alone in my obsession. After all, he is one of the bestselling recording artists of all time. Without him there is no Cure, U2, Lou Reed, Joy Division, LCD Soundsystem, or even Lady Gaga. *Rolling Stone* magazine recently called him "the greatest rock star who ever fell to this or any other world."[1]

But with Bowie, the main attraction was never just "Changes" or "Ashes to Ashes"; it was Bowie—or Ziggy Stardust, Aladdin Sane, the Thin White Duke, or one of his endless supply of alter egos. Before he was Bowie, David Robert Jones was a struggling musician moving from band to band and churning out a string of singles nobody bought. Even after he changed his name to David Bowie, his first solo album went nowhere—and it's easy to see why. In those years, Bowie was still trying to fit into existing categories of what he thought people wanted him to be. Whether he was playing blues covers or folk, it all sounded like something people had already heard. It was all too familiar.

And guess what? Nobody wanted anything to do with that David Bowie.

But by 1969, when he dropped "Space Oddity" days before the launch of NASA's Apollo 11, he was on his way to becoming an international rock god that would change the shape of popular culture forever. In the decade that followed, he went on a creative tear unequaled in the history of rock. From the albums *The Man Who Sold the World*, *Hunky Dory*, and *The Rise and Fall of Ziggy Stardust and the Spiders from Mars* on through to *Young Americans*, *Heroes*, and the posthumous release of the haunting masterpiece *Blackstar*, Bowie was constantly reinventing himself, incorporating new ideas, pushing boundaries, and challenging assumptions every chance he got—even from beyond the grave.

The timing of this renaissance was no accident. Bowie spent the two years between his first failed solo album and the release of "Space Oddity" discovering new influences and exploring new ways of making art. He lived at a Buddhist monastery, studied dance, drama, and mime, and helped create an experimental arts lab.[2] He was finding ways to be his true self and express it better. He went deep into himself so that he could understand what he wanted to say and convince all of us to pay attention.

Most of all, he found his own vision and learned to always trust it.

What made him irresistible as an artist is that he wasn't trying to be the next Jagger or Dylan. He was becoming the first and only David Bowie, a man to whom old categories just didn't apply. He wasn't blues or pop, psychedelic or soul, man or woman, gay or straight. He didn't have a single identity. What united everything he did was that it came from David Bowie being an original. And that was enough.

Growing up outside of Washington, D.C., in conservative Fairfax County, Virginia, I would pore over Bowie's every album, lyric, and persona. I didn't always know what I was feeling when I listened to a Bowie track, but I knew I felt something *soulful*. And it was way more interesting than the band Wham!

At the time I discovered Bowie, I was already the semi–black sheep of my family. My parents and a lot of my relatives are teachers and academics. My interests were incomprehensible to them. I was not a bookworm; I was a shameless television addict obsessed with *Knight Rider* and *The Greatest American Hero*. I also loved watching the thirty-second stories sprinkled between the TV shows. I still think about ads like "Oh yeah!" from the Kool-Aid Man, "How many licks does it take to get to the Tootsie Roll center of a Tootsie Pop?" or "Leggo my Eggo"—a tagline that my sister and I repeated countless times at the breakfast table. Even today I find myself saying "Time to make the donuts"—from the Dunkin' Donuts ads of my childhood—when I head off to work. I would break down every component of these old ads, from the music to the acting to the direction, analyzing what made them work. Did that ad persuade me to buy the thing they were hawking? This was definitely not normal behavior for a twelve-year-old, certainly not in my family of intellectuals and educators.

It took David Bowie to show me that weirdness isn't something to fight against—it's something to wrap your arms around. Bowie gave me license to be my own strange and unique self.

Ironically, Bowie's first and only office job was as an artist at Nevin D. Hirst Advertising in London.[3] He washed out of that gig pretty quickly. But even later on, he maintained a close relationship with the advertising world, appearing in TV spots for everything from Pepsi to Louis Vuitton.[4]

It may sound counterintuitive that I learned the importance of authenticity from David Bowie—the master of self-creation, the man of endless identities—but it makes sense. Yes, he was a mess of contradictions and radically different personalities, but it was all original and true to Bowie every single time. You may not have understood what he was up to, but you knew he was showing you a unique side of himself and that he didn't care what anyone else thought. You felt it in your bones.

And that quality of being authentically yourself is at the heart of all persuasion.

## Character Is King

Persuasion is about personal character, not facts or argument. The most powerful modes of persuasion don't have much to do with evidence, argument, or logic. In fact, often what persuades people isn't the substance of what's being said but the source—in other words, the person saying it. Aristotle knew this more than two millennia ago. As he put it, "We believe good men more fully and more readily than others . . . [A speaker's] character may almost be called the most effective means of persuasion he possesses."[5]

This makes sense. On most issues, we just don't have the knowledge, time, or expertise to figure out on our own which side to take. I trust my doctor when he tells me I need to take vitamin D supplements or to stay off my sprained ankle for a week. It isn't the science that convinces me—I didn't go to medical school and I have no idea why we need so much damn vitamin D, but my doctor went to medical school and studied to know her craft, and the good ones project the conviction and character to make us listen.

When a politician tries to persuade you about tax reform or national security or immigration, most of the time you don't have enough information to decide based on the facts alone.

You're deciding based on whether or not this person seems well intentioned, trustworthy, confident, and sincere. You're deciding based on the individual's perceived character.

What I mean by character—or, more important, what Aristotle meant—isn't just the list of ethical rules you try to follow or the personal beliefs you hold. Your character is also made up of the habits and dispositions that you display without thinking. When a brave person sees a burning school, they don't hesitate to run into the building to help the kids inside. When an honest person finds a lost wallet, they do their best to return it to its owner and don't consider for a second taking the cash inside. A sincere person tells the truth reflexively, not after weighing the pros and cons of being truthful.

So the character traits that make you persuasive also need to flow from your core. People need to know that they're getting a glimpse of the real you—a peek at something that you don't even know that you're showing them.

## Peep Show of the Soul

The first step in developing a persuasive character is learning to be unapologetically yourself.

I know, I know, "Be yourself" is nothing fresh. You've heard it a million times. It's something you say to a friend who's preparing for a job interview or about to ask someone out on a date. But what people usually mean when they say "Be yourself" is "Relax, be natural, and don't overthink it."

That's not what I'm talking about, because in most situations where we are trying to be persuasive, our instincts lead us in the wrong direction. We try to hide those parts of ourselves that we assume the other person won't appreciate. And we say and do things we think will make us more attractive to our audience. We smile more than usual or act excited about something we don't really care about. We speak in more formal language than we normally do in real life. Put simply, we try to fake it till we make it.

But that's not what human beings respond to. They can see what you're doing from a mile away, whether they realize it or not. Recent experiments by researchers Leanne ten Brinke, Dayna Stimson, and Dana R. Carney at the University of California, Berkeley's Haas School of Business demonstrate just how amazing we are at unconsciously detecting bullshit.[6] Their work set out to discover whether split-second, gut-level reactions were better at identifying dishonesty than our conscious judgment. To do this, the researchers conducted an experiment in which they asked a group of undergraduates to look at videotaped interrogations of people suspected of stealing $100. Only some of the suspects actually stole the money. But every person videotaped was told to deny that they were guilty. Some actually had done it, but everyone denied it.

Surprisingly, when the undergraduates were asked to *consciously* identify which suspects were lying and which were telling the truth, their answers weren't very accurate. In fact, they managed only 54 percent accuracy, just barely better than if they guessed.

Here's what's incredible: When the researchers measured the undergraduates' *unconscious* split-second gut reactions to the videos, the students proved much better at sorting the liars from the truth-tellers. Specifically, participants who were thinking about one of the videotaped liars responded faster to words like "dishonest," "deceitful," and "untruthful" than to words like "honest" or "genuine" during a test designed to measure automatic mental reactions. When they were thinking about one of the truthful suspects, the opposite was true.[7, 8]

In other words, what Brinke, Stimson, and Carney's work was showing us is that people are pretty impressive at detecting dishonesty with split-second, gut-level accuracy—way better than they are at consciously calling bullshit. So when you tell little white lies to get in your audience's good graces, there's a good chance you'll end up tripping their deception alarm right off the bat, without their even thinking about it. They may not know exactly what you're hiding, but they'll know you're hiding something. And once they get even a whiff of insincerity, you become just another salesperson trying to put one over on them.

There are two ways to get around someone's built-in bullshit sensor. First, you can learn to be an expert bullshitter. It's not easy, but people can certainly do it. They're called con artists. And if you'd like to become one, there are other books out there for you. This isn't one of them.

For those of us who enjoy sleeping well at night, there's another option: stop trying to get people to like you and start being fully who you are. Or, to put it differently, don't be David Robert Jones when he was making the by-the-numbers music he thought people wanted. Be Ziggy Stardust, and put your weirdest, most honest, and wonderful self out there, even if that means violating a few social norms.

I'll give you a personal example. For years I pretended to like wine. I've been to Napa probably a few dozen times. And each time I followed the drill: I swished and spat. I held my glass up to the light and swirled it around. I used words like "oaky" and "full-bodied" like I knew what I was talking about. I memorized some of the regions and the varietals and which wine pairs with which food. I thought I was super-bougie.

I convinced myself that I enjoyed all of this, but I really didn't. I actually hate wine. It's acidic. It makes my teeth turn purple. And after drinking it, wine makes me want to go knock out. I am more of a high-energy guy. I'll take a mescal or vodka cocktail any night of the week (every night during some tough weeks). I just felt like wine was the kind of thing I was supposed to like, so I went with the flow—especially when I was with someone I wanted to impress.

These days, when I sit down at a restaurant, I hand my wine-glass back to the waiter first chance I get. It turns out that people respect that. The wine lovers I know respect it the most, because they definitely don't want to spend all night listening to a poseur recite some pretentious bullshit he tried to learn in Napa. Plus, it means there's more wine for them.

Turning off your filter and showing a little psychic skin can give you a real leg up when you're trying to sway your audience. There are a number of reasons why this works. First, an original human being—with real likes and dislikes, out-there interests, and surprising obsessions—is something other people can recognize and relate to, whether they fully identify with that person or not.

After all, diversity is the one thing we have in common.

Also, you become memorable, a known quantity, and that makes you far more trustworthy than someone who seems to be putting on a show. It also gives you a chance to share a part of yourself and tell personal stories.

I'm shameless about filling the walls of my office with images of artists, musicians, and historical figures whom I truly love and am inspired by. Sure, the client I'm trying to land might hate The Clash or Prince, but she almost certainly loves some kind of music or art or cultural icon. That makes the picture of Joe Strummer something she can relate to, and it helps make me into a human being instead of a businessperson trying to get something out of her.

But there's another reason to put your whole, authentic self out there whenever possible: it's almost impossible to anticipate what parts of your identity other people will be drawn to. You might think that your collection of tiny porcelain cats, ski resort shot glasses, retro Nike sneakers, Marvel comic books, or whatever you're obsessed with will be incomprehensible to your audience, but it might be exactly the thing that they appreciate most about you. And it makes you memorable. On top of that, the fact that you opened yourself up to scrutiny conveys confidence. And when it comes to persuasion, confidence is power.

When you let your freak flag fly, it shows the other person that they are trusted, respected, and welcome. And you also welcome hearing about their unique interests and obsessions.

That's why it pays to be your strangest self. But here's the tricky part: none of these reasons should be on your mind when you're actually seeking to persuade someone. If you're only putting yourself out there in order to make a sale, then you're not being genuine—you're being manipulative. You need to get to a place where the uniqueness you show in your interactions comes from someplace real. It needs to be something you do without thinking. Letting people in on your quirks makes you interesting and memorable. Who wants to blend in and be bland and forgettable?

It comes easily to some people—and it becomes easier with age—but it usually takes awareness, discipline, and practice. Not even Bowie did it naturally—he had to go off and learn how to do it.

## How to Have More Authentic Interactions

How do you learn to be even more of an original? Sounds like a trick question, but it's not. In fact, there is a simple method you can put into daily action. It comes down to three steps.

### Awareness

Awareness in this case is really listening to what you're saying. Start by paying more attention to every interaction you have. What you're looking for are instances when you say or do something that doesn't reflect what you truly feel. Maybe you gave a half laugh at somebody's off-color attempt at humor. Maybe you pretended to be way more happy or pissed-off by today's weather than you really are. Maybe you stopped yourself from sharing something about yourself because you weren't sure how the other person would react or feel about you.

Most of us do these things automatically. And sure, each instance might be innocent enough. You're just being polite, you tell yourself. Or you're just trying to avoid confrontation, finish this awkward conversation, and get on with your life. But these little moments of insincerity can quickly add up to full-blown phoniness. At the very least, they are missed opportunities to show something about yourself that's real.

Moments like these take different forms in each person, but once you know what you're looking for, they're hard to miss.

So when you see yourself engaging in this kind of small-scale insincerity, take note.

## Analysis: Do a Postgame Breakdown

Just like an athlete looks at game tape to keep their skills sharp, you'll want to do a postgame analysis on your personal exchanges or pitches to see where you can be more yourself. After each conversation is over, ask yourself whichever of these questions applies:

- Where in that conversation was I being my most genuine self?

- Where did I notice myself being insincere or holding back?

With that information in hand, ask:

- How can I build on those moments where I was letting myself show through?

For the less genuine moments, ask:

- What would I have said or done if I was being honest? If I was being my most genuine self? If I wasn't so concerned about how the other person saw me?

- How would I have acted if I was talking to my oldest friend—someone who knows me better than I know myself?

Don't get me wrong—I'm not telling you to be an insulting asshole just for the sake of standing out. If your answer to any of these questions is "You're sucking the life out of me! Please stop talking!," you've missed the point. Your goal isn't to get the other person to take a swing at you. It's just to conduct the conversation as genuinely as possible.

## Adaptation: Implement What You've Learned

However you answer those questions, you need to put this knowledge into action. Keep a journal where you record your strengths and weaknesses. Perhaps there's a conversation topic that really brings out your most genuine self. Or maybe there's a detail about your life that you go to great lengths not to talk about—maybe you even seek to conceal it. People respect you when you tell them deeply personal things about your life. You might have things you say without thinking, or things you pretend to like that you hate. Don't be ashamed of your experiences and points of view; be proud of them.

The simple act of writing them down will help you internalize these lessons. And if you get into the habit of doing this, you'll become much more deeply aware of when you're being phony. Over time, you'll begin catching yourself before the words leave your mouth, until eventually it will become automatic.

It's just like learning a musical instrument—say, piano. At first, you have to think about every single detail: the way you sit, where your feet are, how much tension is in your wrists, your fingering, the tempo, how hard to strike each key. Every note you play takes intense concentration. But as you master the instrument, more and more of what you do just becomes purely automatic. At that point, the music just seems to pour out of you. Or, even better, it's like learning a foreign language. At first you have to obsess about grammar, vocabulary, and tense.

You conjugate verbs in your head and carefully pronounce each word. You flip through a dictionary and memorize words. But once you master the language, all of that falls away and the words flow directly from your mind without hesitation.

This is the process that you should apply to developing every persuasive habit detailed in this book. Don't think of it as having to learn something new. Think of it as discovering and leaning into the unique qualities that are already in you.

It's what golfers mean when they talk about "finding their swing." They're not engineering a perfect swing from scratch so much as they're discovering their natural swing through deliberate practice. And, in a way, this will help you find *your* swing.

## Collect Role Models and Study Them

There will be times when you're tired or hungry or just uninterested in self-improvement. What's lacking in these instances is inspiration. And a reliable way to deal with flagging inspiration is to have a collection of role models you can turn to.

Specifically, you should always be on the lookout for people you admire for their sincere, no-bullshit demeanor. Could be Steve McQueen. Could be Oprah. Could be Steph Curry. Could be the person who cuts your hair. Doesn't matter, as long as it works for you.

Now think about why, exactly, they come off the way they do. Look closely at the way they speak, their tone, their use of eye contact, their choice of words, conversation topics—all of it. Here too, I recommend you keep a journal where you can riff on the character traits that you admire. My ode to Bowie earlier in the chapter comes right from my notebook.

By doing this, you're internalizing those features of your role models that you find most admirable so that you can draw on them in your own life. And in times when you feel yourself slipping into people-pleasing mode, think back to one of these figures and picture how they would act in your situation. Your goal isn't to copy the idiosyncrasies of these individuals but to be inspired by them.

## Why "Be Confident" Is Horrible Advice

Confident people are naturally persuasive—you don't need me to tell you that. If two mechanics give me conflicting reports on what's wrong with my car, I'm going with the one who says he knows for sure that my problem is a blown head gasket. I'm definitely not putting my money on the guy who sounds like he's guessing. And, the science bears this out.

In one experiment, psychologists Paul C. Price and Eric R. Stone showed a group of thirty-five people the stock predictions of two fictional financial analysts—one named Brown, the other named Green. Participants would learn, for instance, that Brown predicted with 86 percent confidence that a particular stock would increase in value, and then they would learn whether or not Brown was right or wrong. For each analyst, participants saw twenty-four such judgment-outcome pairs, giving them a decent track record for both Brown and Green.[9]

The participants were then asked to choose which analyst they would hire. Now, neither analyst was better at predicting stocks than the other. In fact, both made exactly the same overall predictions on every single stock. The only difference was that one of the analysts was always extremely confident—predicting with 99 percent confidence, say, when his counterpart predicted with 84 percent confidence. Even when the overconfident analyst was uncertain, he was extremely uncertain—giving a prediction with 7 percent confidence instead of the other analyst's 22 percent confidence.

Sure enough, participants overwhelmingly preferred the more confident analyst, even though he wasn't any better at picking stocks. When faced with two equally good options, confidence makes the difference.

This suggests that there's a good reason people often tell you to "be confident" if your intention is to persuade. But I'm not going to do that. Because the truth is, "be confident" is bad advice. The next time someone says it to you, do yourself a favor and ignore them. Telling people to "be confident" is like telling them to "be sleepy" or "be surprised"—you can't just decide to do it. What you *can* decide to do is *project* confidence. Or, more precisely, you can adopt habits and develop character traits that will make your confidence real.

Being comfortable in your own skin is more than half the battle when it comes to conveying confidence. But there are also a number of more specific strategies for communicating more confidently.

## Speaking Truth with Power

If you're going to say something, say it. If you're not willing to state an important idea without a bunch of qualifications, then don't say it. Stop using language that waters down what we're saying or suggests uncertainty. I'm talking about words and phrases like:

- maybe
- probably
- sort of
- I think
- I could be wrong
- I feel like . . .
- This might be a stupid idea, but . . .

Just get rid of them. The same goes for throat-clearing introductory comments like "Can I ask you a question?" or "Let me
bounce an idea off you."

These little disclaimers and hedges are what communication
researchers call *powerless speech*, and it's obvious why.[10] When
you speak this way, you broadcast your insecurity to your audi
ence and give the impression that what you're saying doesn't
deserve to be taken seriously. At that point, you can kiss any
chance at persuading them goodbye, because they're not buying
what you're selling. Why would they? You're not even buying
it yourself.

Some might object to this strategy as a kind of deception.
After all, isn't it dishonest to pretend to be more confident than
you really are? Yes. But I'm not telling you to pretend. Only to
change the way you express things that you actually believe.
Because if your speech is littered with powerless language, even
statements you believe in deeply will come off as unbelievable,
or at least questionable. Using powerful language starts to increase your confidence. And using powerless speech does the
same in the opposite direction.

I learned this the hard way. I was recently asked to appear
on a nationally broadcast Fox show to discuss that year's Super
Bowl advertising trends. I was excited to do it. After all, if

there's anything I can discuss with authority, it's the advertising industry. I'm also a die-hard fan of great advertising, so the Super Bowl is like my Christmas—er, Chanukah.

I felt great about the segment while it was happening. Then I saw the footage. Right from the beginning of the interview, my speech was hesitant. Half the words in my first sentence were either "You know, . . ." or "I kinda think that . . ." I felt confident and enthusiastic, but you wouldn't have known it from hearing me. It took about two minutes for me to find my groove, by which time the interview was halfway over.[11]

The interview had to be done remotely from a crowded newsroom, and I couldn't see the person I was talking to. The newscaster mispronounced the name of my agency while she was introducing me, which threw me off my game even further. But little mishaps like that are to be expected, and if that experience taught me anything, it's how easy it is to slip back into bad habits when the pressure is on.

The only way to prevent such episodes from derailing you is to practice. And when it comes to scrubbing your speech of powerless language, you can adopt the same three-step process I outlined previously.

- **AWARENESS:** First, listen for these words and phrases in your everyday speech.

- **ANALYSIS:** Second, spend a minute noticing where you slipped into this kind of talk and thinking about how you could have expressed yourself more directly.

- **ADAPTATION:** Finally, take note of the powerless words you rely on the most, and make a deliberate effort not to use them.

You'll find that cutting out powerless words doesn't change the meaning of what you say one bit. Compare these two sentences and you'll see what I mean:

- **POWERLESS:** "If I'm being honest, I'd have to say that Beyoncé might be one of the greatest live shows of all time, at least in my current opinion."

- **POWERFUL:** "Beyoncé is the greatest live show."

- **POWERLESS:** "Don't get me wrong, I've got nothing against that author. His books just don't really work for me, personally."

- **POWERFUL:** "I don't like that author's style."

People don't need reminding that you're intending to be honest; they don't need to be told that it's you who's saying something; and they certainly understand that it's your opinion that's being expressed. Who else's opinion would it be?

I've found that if you make an effort to use more powerful language, it will actually affect the way you think. You'll begin to formulate thoughts in clear, confident statements, since you no longer have your old linguistic crutches to lean on.

## Be a Daredevil with a Cause

When you take a stand, make sure it's for the right reasons. Going beyond everyday conversations, you will have to take a stand on something you believe in. Making bold statements just for the sake of boldness isn't effective. There's a fine line between confidence and recklessness. And when you do something extreme just to be provocative, it's called a stunt. Nobody trusts a daredevil. I wouldn't take advice from Evel Knievel—unless I wanted to master jumping a motorcycle over fourteen Greyhound buses.

A stunt is done for spectacle. By contrast, when you take a stand on an issue, that choice needs to strike at the heart of who you are and what you believe. It's the difference between a flash mob and a civil rights march: one is pointless, the other inspiring.

If you're going to take a risk, you need to be serving a system of values. To do that, you need to identify what your core values are. By values, I don't just mean your beliefs about politics and your sense of right and wrong, although that's part of it. I'm referring to the things you find most important in life—big ideas like loyalty, optimism, creativity, directness, or beauty. Ask yourself: What are the principles and commitments that you're not willing to compromise, no matter what? You can ask the same about the organization you work for or lead.

Whatever your answer, that's what should be motivating you when you make a gutsy decision or express a strong view. Even if that choice doesn't pan out, it will have come from someplace true. And that's something people can respect regardless of the outcome.

Bowie didn't paint a lightning bolt across his face and call himself Ziggy Stardust for the hell of it. He was trying to advance a creative vision and to explore new ways of making art that were true to his original self.

 # RECAP

The goal is to get to a place where the things you do and say reflect the real you. When you're speaking from your gut, you're not worrying about how other people are perceiving you, and that's a real achievement. If you're contorting yourself into something you hope people will like, the only person you'll end up fooling is yourself. One thing I've learned during my career in advertising is that your audience's ability to sense deception far outstrips your ability to deceive them.

The methods I've found to avoid this kind of insincerity are:

1. Put your true self out there.
2. Speak and act with confidence.
3. Collect role models.
4. Boldly follow your core values.

If you do this, your true character will shine through in ways you could have never anticipated.

Confidence is feeling safe to be yourself. And that comes from conviction and knowing who you are. There's more to developing a soulfully persuasive character than being your original self, but without this basic personality trait in place, you won't have much luck persuading others.

As the graphic designer Sean McCabe has put it, you will never influence the world by trying to be like it.[12]

# the persuasive power of storytelling

---

*There's always room for a story that can transport people to another place.*

—J. K. Rowling

When people ask what I do for a living—or what my company, Mekanism, does—my response is always the same: *storytelling.* Yes, we're an advertising agency. So, at the end of the day, we are in the business of selling products, whether it's ice cream, sneakers, or deodorant. But the way we go about this task is to figure out a brand's core truth and tell *stories* that communicate that truth in compelling, resonant, and entertaining ways.

This approach is a lot different from the way advertisers used to sell products. Until a few decades ago, it was standard practice for ads to list the benefits and features of the latest car or cleaning product or household appliance and brag about its "low, low price." In effect, advertisements straight-up told consumers why it was a good idea to buy something. The only thing ads were supposed to do was give you the facts (even if those facts were slightly stretched).

But in today's world, you have to relate to your audience in a more emotional, truthful, and soulful way if you want to make a connection. In this arena, facts and features alone simply don't have what it takes. It's storytelling that moves, connects, and creates meaningful bonds between brands and consumers. It's storytelling that holds the greatest power of persuasion—and not just in the world of advertising.

Researchers have long recognized storytelling as a universal—and beneficial—human activity going back to the earliest days of our species. As the historian Yuval Noah Harari writes, "The real difference between us and chimpanzees is the mysterious glue that enables millions of humans to cooperate effectively. This mysterious glue is made of stories, not genes."[1]

So, yes, we kind of owe our very existence to storytelling. Research by anthropologist Daniel Smith of University College London and his team found that storytelling "may have played an essential role in the evolution of human cooperation by broadcasting social and cooperative norms to coordinate group behavior."[2] We tell stories to communicate our values and compel others to adopt those same values.

There's a good reason we've been using stories to persuade each other since our earliest days: more than any other form of communication, stories have the power to inspire loyalty, to take us out of the present moment and let us consider ideas from a fresh perspective, and to make us understand things on an emotional level. So if your goal is to change minds and move people to action, a proficiency in storytelling is a basic necessity.

I will explore what exactly makes stories such a powerful tool of persuasion. But we can also reveal the habits and character traits that can enable anyone to become a persuasive storyteller.

## From Presidents to Paris: Swaying Through Story

When told well, a great story draws people into the narrative, absorbing them in a world that is separate from their own and creating an almost supernatural connection with the main characters. For a brief moment in time, the audience forgets themselves and begins to inhabit the story. You've experienced this yourself while watching an engrossing movie or getting lost in a novel. And once you're immersed in a story, you're far more willing to let your guard down and loosen your grip on preconceived notions.

It's no coincidence that the great religions of the world conveyed their messages through myth, allegory, and biblical stories. Or that the greatest leaders of our time have also been some of the world's best storytellers, whether it was Martin Luther King Jr., Mahatma Gandhi, the Notorious RBG, or Nelson Mandela.

Perhaps the greatest practitioner of persuasive storytelling in American history was Abraham Lincoln. "They say I tell a great many stories," Lincoln once said. "I reckon I do; but I have learned from long experience that plain people . . . are more easily influenced through the medium of a broad and humorous illustration than in any other way."[3]

For Stephen Douglas, his famous opponent in the historic Lincoln–Douglas Debates over the institution of slavery, Lincoln's storytelling ability was something to be feared. "Every one of his stories seems like a whack upon my back," Douglas once remarked. "Nothing else, not any of his arguments or any of his replies to my questions disturbs me. But when he begins to tell a story, I feel that I am to be overmatched."[4]

Even Lincoln's most famous speech, the Gettysburg Address, is presented to transport people to the founding of our nation, "four score and seven years ago."

Near the end of the Civil War, the president was asked by General William Tecumseh Sherman how the military should deal with Confederate president Jefferson Davis. Lincoln's main concern was holding the Union together in the wake of this bloody war and ensuring that those who fought for the other side returned to American society peacefully.

Publicly punishing Davis would have inflamed political tensions throughout the country. But letting Davis off the hook would have been just as toxic politically. As Lincoln saw it, the best-case scenario for a country ripped apart at the seams was for the former Confederate president to escape the country. Of course, Lincoln couldn't make these wishes known publicly, so he expressed his position with a story. It involved a man who had given up drinking. When the man was asked by a friend whether he'd like a drink of alcohol, he declined and requested a glass of lemonade. As the friend poured the lemonade, he mentioned that the beverage would taste better with a little brandy in it. The man explained that if the brandy was added without his knowledge, he wouldn't object. Sherman got the point: Lincoln wanted the general to let Davis escape, but without the president knowing.[5]

Without this capacity for storytelling, it's unlikely Lincoln would have been able to build the political network—or the popular support—that allowed him to become president. (Incidentally, stories may have been more than mere persuasive tools for Lincoln. Some suspect that the funny and lighthearted anecdotes he told were a way to manage his own debilitating depression—a way for him to try to rewire his own brain.)

Luckily, you don't have to be a master politician of Lincoln's magnitude to use storytelling to your advantage. Consider a situation in which you're trying to convince your partner to vacation in Paris instead of London. You might point out that Paris has world-class food, unrivaled museums, and better weather than London. But again, from the point of view of persuasion—like advertising—just listing benefits and features isn't a very effective way to win someone over.

At best, telling someone why they should do something—buy a product, vote for someone, donate to a charity—appeals to their intellect. It invites them to weigh the pros and cons of a situation and reason their way to a logical conclusion. That's fine. But logic is only part of the puzzle, and argument is rarely the best way to change minds.

At worst, this approach will spark a confrontation. After all, nobody likes being told what to do, as anybody who has ever raised a child knows all too well. And if your audience already has a serious stake in their current position, preaching to them about why they are wrong can make them dig in their heels even more.

Now imagine that, instead of listing the reasons your partner should pick Paris over London, you went to a screening of Jean-Luc Godard's *Breathless*, or, if French New Wave isn't your cup of tea, Woody Allen's *Midnight in Paris*, Richard Linklater's *Before Sunset*, or some other movie that shows Paris in all of its romantic beauty and transports you to those picturesque streets.

The fact is, that experience will do far more to convince your significant other than any list of tourist attractions, as stories engage us on a deep emotional level.

For me, the most formative example of the persuasive power of great storytelling comes from one of the most mediocre bands of all time: Kiss. Yes, I am talking about the makeup-covered, high-heel-wearing, fire-breathing, tongue-waving performance-based rock band.

## How Kiss Used Storytelling to Win Over the World

As a kid, I couldn't get enough of Kiss. I mean, these guys were from another planet. They wore crazy black leather costumes. They set things on fire and played instruments that floated in the air. They even spat up blood. I blasted every album, from *Dressed to Kill* to *Destroyer*. I learned every (pedestrian) lyric, and frequently covered my face in black and white greasepaint. And, of course, my parents raised their eyebrows and shook their heads when I emerged from my room waggling my tongue and holding up devil horns.

Whereas Bowie was a bona fide musical genius, the members of Kiss almost certainly were not. Don't get me wrong—the music was always a good time, even if it was basic. Yet somehow, despite their lack of talent as musicians, the band produced a total of thirty gold albums. That's more than any other American band in history, according to the Recording Industry Association of America. Fourteen of their albums went platinum, and three went multi-platinum.[6]

Kiss's success went far beyond record sales. The band inspired a following unlike any other musical act before them. We go by the name "Kiss Army" and, among other things, we take it upon ourselves to call up radio stations and harass DJs into playing the band's music. This brilliant approach to marketing is something I've since adopted in my own work in advertising. But back then, I didn't see it as marketing—I saw it as an act of devotion for a band that drew me in. I was just thrilled to be a small part of their huge community. In a way, the Kiss Army was the world's first influencer network. The fans built the band.

Kiss was also a pioneer in the realm of branded merchandise, producing a seemingly endless supply of outlandish swag. Kiss managed to slap their image on everything from action figures and comic books to lip balm, pocket knives, money clips, condoms, coffins, and even bank checks.[7] Imagine how devoted to the band you have to be to pay your rent with a Kiss-branded check.

How do you explain this level of popularity from a band that, musically speaking, was far from brilliant? How did they inspire an army of followers and sell so many albums without even producing a number one hit single in the United States?[8] Simple: it was all about storytelling. Whether it was Gene Simmons's long-tongued monster or drummer Peter Criss's "Catman," Paul Stanley's' "Starchild," or Ace Frehley's "Spaceman," these guys weren't musicians. They were psychotic demons from some alien mythology of their own invention. In other words, they were characters in an immersive story that I and millions of others found irresistible. Their music was simply a vehicle for transporting their audience into their deranged and exhilarating narrative.

Before they created this story, they were just some average-looking long-haired rockers from New York City who could barely get an audience to fill up a local bar. Once they invented their alternate world of story, however, it no longer mattered. In fact, you didn't even notice the music. You only noticed the story they were telling.

This kind of deep, non-rational connection with one's audience is something that only great storytelling can achieve. That's why stories are such a powerful tool for shaping people's views, forging allegiances, and changing minds: they grant you access to a part of the human psyche that logical argumentation simply can't touch. And it's for this reason that learning to become a great storyteller is a critical part of developing a persuasive character.

## Stories Convince Through Transportation

The amazing feeling of being absorbed into a story the way I was as a young soldier in the Kiss Army is such a basic human sensation that psychologists have a term for it: *transportation*. Researchers have found that when we are transported by a story, our brains actually process information differently. We become less aware of the real world, and more aware of the world of the story. And sure enough, this makes us more open to altering our beliefs. In a way, scientists are finally discovering a truth that Gene Simmons knew back in the 1970s.

A study by social psychologists Melanie C. Green and Timothy C. Brock offers some compelling proof of the power of transportation. The researchers conducted several experiments in which participants were asked to read an admittedly disturbing story. In it, a young girl named Katie goes to a shopping mall with her older sister, Joan, and ends up being brutally stabbed to death by an escaped psychiatric patient. Pretty gruesome stuff, sure. But that was the point. For the experiments to work, researchers needed a story that was emotionally engaging. The story was also designed to communicate a set of beliefs, although only implicitly. For instance, the narrative implies that shopping malls aren't safe, that psychiatric patients need better supervision, and that the world is just a shitshow.

What Green and Brock found over the course of several experiments was that readers who scored high on levels of transportation tended to adopt beliefs that were more consistent with the story—such as that psychiatric patients need more supervision. Highly transported readers also showed more positive feelings toward the story's protagonists. Readers who for whatever reason were less transported had fewer story-consistent beliefs and less love for the main characters. Remarkably, these results weren't much affected by whether or not the story was presented as fiction or fact.[9]

Now, imagine what you would have to do to convince someone that shopping malls aren't safe or that psych patients need more supervision if you were using nothing but logical argument. You'd need to bring forth evidence, whether in the form of statistics or expert testimony. And you'd have to somehow demonstrate why your research proves your conclusion. You might organize all of this in a PowerPoint presentation, with line graphs and bullet points.

Let's assume that your audience manages to sit through this slideshow without dozing off. (As someone who has been subjected to hundreds of PowerPoint presentations, I can say that's not a safe assumption.) After all of this, your audience might end up agreeing with you. But there is a strong chance that, based on their own experiences at shopping malls or in psych wards, they wouldn't.

Why? For starters, charts and bullet points alone can be a snoozefest. And paying attention to them usually requires a tremendous amount of focus. So right off the bat, you're asking your audience to do you a favor by even listening. That's not a good note to start on if your goal is to persuade them. Data is important, but it is just part of the equation.

A great story, on the other hand, doesn't take a lot of work or discipline to pay attention to. It pulls you in automatically, whether you want it to or not. They're actually interesting to listen to—more like entertainment than work. And this makes them a lot easier to remember. In fact, information that is presented in stories is up to twenty-two times more memorable than straight facts.[10]

When you persuade through storytelling, you don't have to hit your audience over the head with your main point. As Green and Brock's shopping mall experiments make clear, it's enough for a story to just imply your main points, and the audience will get there on their own—so long as you give them the opportunity to do so. That's crucial, because conclusions that we draw for ourselves will always be more powerful than the ones we are forced to accept. The beliefs I arrive at on my own are mine—they belong to me personally. And as a result, I'm usually much less willing to give them up when push comes to shove. That's why, when I need to convey an idea to my clients, colleagues, and employees, I usually have a story on hand to go along with the data, to get the message across.

## Using Stories to Convey Values:
## A Cautionary Tale by Walt Disney

My advertising agency, Mekanism, is a company devoted to selling brands through storytelling. That's the service we provide to our clients. My role as CEO at the agency relies on effective storytelling.

It's my job to sell ideas to clients and persuade them that our work will resonate with their intended audience. When they're dead set on a bad strategy, I try to talk them out of it. And if they're not sure if they should hire us, I explain why we're the right agency for the job. In every one of these instances it's up to me and the team to tell a story that helps persuade the clients.

But there's another aspect of my job for which storytelling is critical: motivating my team and rallying them around our agency's core values and beliefs. One of our core values is collaboration. Mekanism prides itself on being an organization that cherishes talented people from a wide range of different backgrounds and disciplines. But it's not enough to collect a bunch of highly skilled people, close your eyes, and hope for the best. Doing truly great work demands that the members of this diverse group complement one another and are able to work together without egos, toward common goals, while adhering to a common set of beliefs.

Now, when I state this idea plainly, as I just did, it might make sense. Or it might just sound like a bunch of touchy-feely nonsense, depending on your perspective. So when I need to communicate the value of collaboration and teamwork to my company, I often reach for a story from Mekanism's early days.

It's about the very first time that my partner—Mekanism's founder and chief creative officer, Tommy Means—and I pitched together. The client was a little company called Disney. At the time, Mekanism was still a small, five- or six-person agency struggling to make a name for ourselves. For this pitch, we teamed up with two Bay Area advertising luminaries, Vince Engel and Wayne Buder. They were both hugely influential in my career. Well connected, they were in the door at Disney.

For a young, hungry company still wet behind the ears, an audience with senior Disney executives was a big deal. This was especially true for Mekanism, because at the time we were running on fumes financially. If we closed Disney, it wouldn't just solve our money troubles, it would rocket us into the big leagues by marking us with the coveted Disney stamp of approval.

Our brief was to design a campaign for the company's Imagineering division. The Imagineers are an elite group of designer-engineers who are responsible for the overall look and feel of everything Disney does in the physical world—resorts, theme parks, rides, hotels, water parks, concert halls, cruise ships. Within Disney, the Imagineers are treated like mystical shamans. And it was our job to bring the Imagineers to life and reveal to an audience of kids the process by which they make their ideas into reality.

Our concept was a cast of animated characters, each of whom illustrated a key aspect of the Imagineering process.

So for instance, there was Spark—a funny-looking little guy with a body resembling a spark plug. Spark produces ideas that appear like a zap of lightning from the electrode at the top of his head. Another character, Fable, is a writer with a keyboard for a lap and a computer screen for a chest. She captures Spark's ideas in poetic writing, after which an artist character, Sketch, turns them into animations. Two more characters, Rock and Block, would take these ideas and build them into the famous rides and attractions at the Disney parks. You get the gist. We thought it was pretty damn brilliant. And it was.

The pitch took place at Disney's headquarters in Burbank, and our audience consisted of three of the most powerful and knowledgeable executives in the entertainment industry at the time: Michael Mendenhall, Disney's chief marketing officer; Leslie Ferraro, vice president of theme parks; and Jay Rasulo, a savvy, hardworking, and decisive executive who oversaw not only Imagineering but also the theme parks and cruise lines, and would eventually become the company's CFO and the number two to CEO Bob Iger.

Rasulo entered the conference room after Ferraro and Mendenhall in full executive mode: power suit and tie, an entourage of assistants taking notes of every syllable he uttered, a "don't fuck with me" expression etched on his face. Then with the simple wave of a hand, the assistants vanished. It was showtime.

With so much on the line, our anxieties were at a fever pitch. So I made the introductions and tried to cut the tension with some allegory about the importance of the Imagineers. Then Tommy, Vince, Wayne, and I launched into our pitch. We had created a timeline board that was the size of the conference room table—so big, in fact, that we had to rent a minivan to get it to the Disney lot. The board said "Imagineers Rollout" across the top. We laid this monstrosity on the table and began to Velcro key elements of the story onto the timeline to show how, where, and when we would tell our Imagineering story to the world.

We explained our idea—to take advantage of Disney's reputation for great characters and storytelling to give the public a peek behind the scenes at Imagineering. We would use experiential elements, comic books, a partnership with the children's literature publisher Scholastic, and digital shorts. We would promote the story at strategic locations within Disney's parks to entertain people waiting in line for rides. I mean, we had about as many brand extensions as Kiss had. We teased the overall concept and got the executives' mouths watering at the possibilities for merchandise and other revenue-driving opportunities. We weren't just creating stories; we were set on creating products.

Then we unveiled the characters. We had spent a good amount of money on prototype action figures, boxes and all, which we ordered specially from a toy manufacturer in China. Now, Tommy is one of the best presenters I have ever seen. He's an expert at captivating a room and telling a great story. So, Tommy, smoothly and like the pitch wizard he is, introduced each Imagineer: Spark, Fable, Sketch, Rock, and Block. We unboxed them and put them on the conference room table next to our huge storytelling calendar. We were on one side. The Disney executives were on the other. And our freshly made characters were staring right up from the table into Rasulo's eyes.

Rasulo's expression softened and his first reaction was encouraging. "I'm not impressed by a lot," he said, "but this is very, very impressive." His next words made it clear that he wasn't totally sold, though. "My only problem is these characters look like robots and kids want characters that look like them. They need to reflect the audience. They want to see human faces, not robots. What do you think about that?"

I could smell victory. And for me, this was an easy criticism to deal with. I'd been in dozens of meetings like this, and I knew from experience that if this was the only problem they had with the idea, we were in great shape. We would nod, explain that these were just rough prototypes, and say something like, "Who are we to tell Disney how to design their characters? These are just thought-starters for us to work on with you. This is a proof of concept."

But Tommy felt bold at this point, and he just wasn't having it. He took the stance of defending the work. And before I could get a word out, he had his say: "That doesn't seem right. These are the characters exactly as we envision them. This explains the Imagineers without having to show the Imagineers." In other words, he was telling them to take it or leave it. He then proceeded to explain why a young creative executive from an agency nobody had heard of yet had a better grasp on what kids would like than three of the top people at the biggest producer of children's entertainment in the history of the world. I tried to kick him under the table, but I couldn't quite reach him with my foot.

At that point, the meeting was over. Jay looked at his watch, pushed his chair back from the table, waved his hand, and mumbled something about "thank you for your presentation, but wrong answer." The gaggle of assistants immediately appeared out of nowhere, and they all walked out as quickly as they had entered. I swear I saw a cartoon cloud swoosh behind them. Clearly, we didn't get the account—or the money.

What went wrong? Put simply, we had failed to collaborate on a key element. In the run-up to the presentation, Tommy let me do my job and I let him do his job, and the result was a genuinely inspired campaign that had a real shot at winning the business and making us and Disney loads of money. We were two young ad guys who were really good at what we did. We trusted each other. But that wasn't enough. We didn't hang together during the pitch. I hadn't prepared how each of us would respond to potential criticisms or questions, the kind of attitude we would convey, or who would say what during this crucial meeting. I didn't properly prep for the Q&A part of the meeting. And, we didn't collaborate when it mattered most. The result was a catastrophe. (We did, however, successfully collaborate on polishing off an overpriced bottle of a fancy Russian vodka at our Burbank hotel later that night.)

## How to Persuade Through Storytelling

Humans are alive today because of our ability to persuade through stories. We have seen how storytelling enabled Lincoln to inspire a nation, and how it turned a mediocre band into a global success—and it's how I am able to keep our company collaborating.

The Disney story has become a piece of agency folklore at Mekanism, a classic internal story about collaboration and preparation, and it's helped us convey the value of collaboration and preparation to hundreds of employees over the years. The reason it works so well is that the story obeys certain fundamental rules of persuasive storytelling.

The steps that follow are basic storytelling, but often serve as a good reminder for anyone.

### Start with a Simple Truth

This one is obvious—if you're trying to communicate an idea with a story, you need to know what that message is before you begin. Great storytellers are also truth-seekers—their aim is to convey an essential human truth through narrative.

In the Disney example, our message was that even if you're

great at your job, failing to prepare as a team can lead to disaster. It's an idea both simple and true.

If you can't state your message in a single uncomplicated sentence, you haven't got one. And if you're trying to communicate more than one message with a single story, then you're likely to lose your audience. Complex stories that allow for multiple interpretations might make for great literature or art, but they aren't good vehicles for persuasive messaging.

## Stick to a Classic Structure

The story also conforms to a basic structure that's as old as storytelling itself. In its simplest form, that structure looks like this:

### The Goal: Who Are Your Characters and What Do They Want?

It starts with a protagonist or several protagonists who want or need something badly. That motivation has to be strong enough to propel the story, and it also needs to be something that your audience can relate to. In the case of Homer's *Odyssey*, Odysseus desperately wants to get home to his family after the Trojan War.

In our example, Tommy and I wanted to land a big account to propel the company. That's our goal in the story: money and success. And it's one that everybody at our agency or any other can easily identify with. It is a universal truth that you have to win business to keep growing.

## The Obstacle: What's in Their Way?

The protagonist(s) then encounter obstacles they must overcome in order to achieve that goal. In our case, we needed to design a great campaign and then we needed to sell it to the folks at Disney during the pitch meeting. By the time you introduce the obstacle, the audience should know what's at stake and what needs to happen, and they should feel some sense of uncertainty. Think of it like telling a joke. What makes a punch line so powerful is the buildup of expectation right before the final reveal. When a punch line lands, it's because the tension created by the setup has been released. The same applies to a great story.

In our example, we had to win this account to be financially safe. Convincing the clients was our obstacle.

## The Resolution: What Is the Outcome?

Either the protagonist(s) overcome their obstacles and achieve their goal or they don't. Regardless, the emotional release that comes at the end of a well-told story should be the most memorable part. So that's when you want your message to become apparent. The protagonist might achieve their goal or they might not, but the way in which they succeed or fail is what will convey your message.

In our example, we didn't succeed—Tommy and I failed to close, specifically because we didn't collaborate in preparing for the wild cards at the end of the pitch. In another universe, we might have landed the account because Rasulo asked a difficult question, Tommy stuck to his guns, and Rasulo loved our bravado. That story would have been about sticking to your convictions and fighting for the creative work.

## How to Be a Great Storyteller

Understanding the basic mechanics of a great persuasive story is one thing. Becoming a great storyteller is another matter entirely. We all know people who can take the most entertaining story you've ever heard and turn it into a dull, confusing mess. You might be one of those people yourself.

If you are, you're not alone. Most people aren't natural-born storytellers, the same way most people aren't natural opera singers or natural graphic artists. Fortunately, great storytelling can be learned through conscious, repeated effort. I am constantly working on it. On that front, here are five techniques that can help you master the fundamentals of persuasive storytelling.

## Technique One: Collect Great Stories

What makes a great story? To some extent, it's the fact that it conforms to the right structure. But really, what separates a decent story from a great story is that it lands your point. It's that special something that makes you excited to repeat it to your friends. In my example, the story is something that employees will want to repeat to new members of the team. It's a juicy bit of gossip in its own right.

Stories like these are all around; you just need to look for them and structure them. Maybe there's an episode from your family history that's particularly entertaining, or something crazy that happened to you on the way to work, or that time you and your friends went to Barcelona. Maybe it's just a story you read or heard or saw on the evening news. Whatever the source, when you happen upon a truly great tale, write it down in as much detail as you can. Keep a notebook or a section of your notebook where you collect these stories.

Once you've got the story on paper, you need to determine what its core message is. Take note of the idea or lesson that the story brings to life. The story might illustrate the importance of keeping promises, or seizing the moment, or doing your holiday shopping late. Regardless, the message should be obvious the first time you hear it. Over time you'll only add to your collection of great stories. And the next time you're trying to make a point about, say, seizing the day, you'll have a great story to draw from.

## Technique Two: Storytelling Is Editing

Once you've found a story that conveys your message and written it out in detail, you still need to make it into something that will hit home with your audience. That means editing. And when getting a story into shape, I like to ask three specific questions.

## Am I Giving My Audience All of the Right Information?

Your listeners probably haven't heard this story before, so make sure you give them all the information they need to understand the action. For instance, look out for crucial characters that appear out of nowhere or technical language that is familiar to you but that your audience might not know.

## Am I Painting a Vivid Enough Picture?

Your goal is to transport your audience, so you need to give them enough specifics to ignite their imagination. This means finding opportunities to add details that bring the story to life. In the Disney story, I mention what the executive was wearing and his entourage of assistants, what some of the characters we created looked like, and the enormous timeline board. You don't want to slow down the action too much, so choose your details wisely. But you also don't want the story to sound like a book report.

## What Can I Cut?

Anything in the story that doesn't help to establish the goal, the obstacle, or the resolution can probably be cut. I didn't go deep into the history of the Imagineers, my first trip to Disneyland as a kid, or my favorite scene from *Fantasia* (which is Mickey as the sorcerer's apprentice—a cautionary tale about cleaning). None of that had anything to do with the three main components of the story structure, so I ditched it.

Now, it's worth noting that I had the luxury of writing it out over several book pages. But most storytelling is spoken. And in my experience, the best spoken stories don't last more than a couple of minutes, tops. So keep that in mind as you're getting your narrative into shape. A good rule of thumb is that it takes a minute to speak 125 words. So if you're writing out the story, it should be no longer than about 250 to 300 words.

## Technique Three: Rehearse

Once you've got a draft that you're happy with, it's time to re-hearse. My process works something like this: First, read it out loud verbatim several times. Your goal isn't to memorize it, but to familiarize yourself with it. When it comes time to tell the story, you don't want it to sound like you're reciting a script. But you do want a firm enough grasp on the basic structure and details that you don't ramble or hesitate.

Next, find yourself a recording device. You'll be surprised what a difference it makes. For starters, the microphone helps to keep you honest. Without a recording device running in the background, it's tempting to rush through your rehearsal, or start over when you get tripped up. But when you've got a voice recorder rolling, it's a lot harder to cheat.

### Memorize Your First and Last Lines

Yes, memorizing your entire story can make it sound lifeless. But it sometimes helps to commit the first and last lines of the story to memory. If you're a little anxious about public speaking, having the first line and the ending locked and loaded will lend you a little extra confidence.

## Technique Four: Learn from the Best

Find examples of storytellers that you admire personally and figure out what makes them great—the same way a great film-maker breaks down the work of a brilliant director, or a great composer studies Mozart's symphonies. You're looking for techniques both large and small that you can apply to your own storytelling. This could be anything from their choice of subject to their tone of voice. Maybe it's the way they transition from one event to the next, the way they start a particular sentence, the use of their hands, the rhythm of a phrase, or the cadence of their voice.

## Technique Five: Don't Overlook Familiar Stories

It's tempting to believe that great stories need to be original—or at least unfamiliar—in order to captivate their audience. But this isn't always the case. In fact, recounting a story that your audience knows already can sometimes be more powerful than telling them one they've never heard. That was the finding of a recent study by psychologists Gus Cooney, Daniel Gilbert, and Timothy D. Wilson.[11]

The researchers conducted a series of experiments involving ninety Harvard undergraduates. In one experiment, participants were split into groups of three. Two students were chosen as listeners while a third was assigned the role of storyteller. The listeners were shown a ten-minute video story—call it video A. In a separate room, the storyteller watched either video A or a different video entirely—call it video B. When the group was reunited, it was up to the storyteller to give a two-minute account of the video he or she had just watched.

Before this happened, however, the storyteller was asked to predict whether the listeners would react more positively to a re-telling of video A, which the listeners had watched, or to video B, a new story that none of the listeners had seen. The majority of the storytellers thought that listeners would enjoy a novel story. But in fact, listeners reacted more negatively to hearing a new story than to hearing one they had just watched. The storytellers, in other words, received what the researchers called a "novelty penalty."[12]

Why would someone enjoy a story they know more than a story they don't? It's a complicated issue. But one of the reasons that Cooney, Gilbert, and Wilson give is that "unlike novel stories, familiar stories activate listeners' memories of their own past experience and are therefore likely to elicit rich emotions."[13]

This makes sense the more you think about it. Some movies are more powerful on the second or third viewing than they are the first time you saw them. And hearing a song you know and love can be a far deeper experience than listening to a song for the first time. Similarly, when your goal is to communicate a message, using a story that listeners already have an emotional connection to can be a huge advantage.

I learned this years and years ago during one of my first experiences as a persuasive storyteller. I had been asked to give a speech at my high school baccalaureate. If you've ever had to sit through one of these commencement-style addresses, then you know that they can easily fall flat or just seem corny, even when the speaker has a genuinely profound piece of wisdom to impart. That danger is even greater when your audience is a group of jaded high school students and their parents.

But I was determined not to let that happen. The message I wanted to get across was simple enough: that our lives are both precious and fleeting, and that we shouldn't let them go to waste. I knew that the best way to communicate this idea was through narrative. So I reached for a story that I knew would be both familiar and emotionally resonant for my audience—Ridley

Scott's dystopian masterpiece *Blade Runner,* based on Philip K. Dick's short novel *Do Androids Dream of Electric Sheep?* The main question *Blade Runner* addresses is "What does it mean to be human?"

The film takes place in a futuristic Los Angeles where artificial humans, known as "replicants," live among us. The main character, Harrison Ford's Deckard, is an ex-cop who works as a "blade runner"—a kind of bounty hunter charged with tracking down and killing these androids.

Much of the audience knew this. Just about every teenager had at least heard of the movie, whether they were sci-fi nerds or not. And a lot of them, like me, were obsessed with it. So I used that familiarity to my advantage by ending my speech with a retelling of the film's iconic final scene.

Deckard is on the run from a highly lethal replicant named Roy, played brilliantly by Rutger Hauer. Roy is desperately trying to stay alive—like a human, he believes that his own life is worth fighting for. While jumping between apartment rooftops in a beautifully cinematic rainstorm, Deckard ends up dangling from the ledge of a building about to fall to his death. At that point, Roy does something unexpected as a replicant—he saves Deckard, the man who is hunting him. The replicant then delivers the film's famous "tears in rain" monologue, which conveys life's precious and fleeting nature more beautifully than anything I could have ever written:

> I've seen things you people wouldn't believe. Attack ships on fire off the shoulder of Orion. I watched C-beams glitter in the dark near the Tannhäuser Gate. All those moments will be lost in time, like tears in rain. Time to die.

Roy's life ends with an act of humanity as he saves the life of Deckard, who had set out to kill him. Even he—an android who was trying to kill his bounty hunter—can't deny the amazing value of a human life. And if an android can see the value and fleetingness of life, then a bunch of high school students shouldn't spend any time wasting theirs.

Those were my final words to our graduating class. My hope was that it would encourage them to experience all that they can in this brief lifetime, just as I was planning on doing. Parents and family members of friends I had never met approached me after the ceremony to tell me they liked the theme. Yet the story wouldn't have been nearly as powerful if those in the audience had never seen or connected to the movie or if it wasn't riding the current pop culture moment. They could see in their minds the scene I was retelling. They were transported.

Just because a story is fairly well known doesn't mean it can't be a great vehicle for conveying a persuasive message. In some situations, familiarity is exactly what's called for.

 **RECAP**

Human beings have been telling stories to one another since our earliest days on the planet—it's one of the reasons we've survived as long as we have. Stories are the way we recount our history and communicate our values; they are how we structure new information and make sense of the world around us.

So when you come across a powerful story, hold on to it—whether it's a personal anecdote or a work of literature, a unique experience or a timeworn piece of popular culture. Make sure it has *the goal*, *the obstacle*, and *the resolution*. And make it your own.

If your goal is to change minds and move people to action, learning to tell compelling, meaningful stories is essential—and will do you far more good than any amount of logical argument. Reason might reveal why we should believe a certain truth. But a well-told story does something even better: it transports us to a place where we can see or experience that truth for ourselves.

As the psychologist Jonathan Haidt puts it, "The human mind is a story processor, not a logic processor."[14]

Chapter 3

# never be closing

---

*Because only one thing counts in this life: get them*
*to sign on the line which is dotted. . . . A-B-C.*
*A—always, B—be, C—closing. Always be closing.*
*Always be closing. . . . Are you interested? I know*
*you are, 'cause it's fuck or walk. You close or you hit*
*the bricks.*

—Blake in *Glengarry Glen Ross*

Thinking and acting in purely transactional terms will sabotage your attempts at persuasion. Sure, persuasion is about getting someone to say yes. But that is short-term thinking and will never add up to genuine persuasion. In order to create the conditions that compel people to side with you, you need to be clear that you care about more than just your own immediate gain.

Being an authentic human being in all of your interactions is essential to developing a persuasive character. Emphasizing your humanity and forging human relationships is what pays real dividends when your goal is to win someone over.

When we are swayed to a particular decision, we're often

evaluating the person delivering the message, their character and motivations, as much as anything else. We're asking ourselves, "Is this person trustworthy?" or "Is this person someone I can see myself doing business with?" or, more often, "What's in it for her?" or "What's his angle here?" If a person's obvious objective is simply to get us to buy something or sign a contract, it will show through, making that person far harder to trust and much less persuasive.

Persuasion isn't about coercing your audience to do what you want. Rather, it's about attracting them to a particular conclusion, and letting them get there on their own. Being pulled is always preferable to being pushed. And one way to draw someone to your position is by engaging your audience's emotions through that most human of activities—storytelling.

We'll now look at personality traits and habits that draw people in by making your interactions about more than the decision at hand—about something *larger*, more long-term, more *human*. In most cases, developing these traits involves avoiding common pitfalls that make our relationships less genuine and more transactional. And that starts by ditching a lot of the conventional wisdom that has come to define persuasion.

## Why "Always Be Closing" Is Always a Mistake

In that classic scene in the 1992 film adaptation of David Mamet's play *Glengarry Glenn Ross*, Alec Baldwin's character, Blake, stands before a room of salesmen and delivers a remedial course on the basics of salesmanship. His takeaway message: "A-B-C. Always be closing." It's a time-honored sales mantra that goes back decades, if not longer. It also happens to be completely wrong.

In fact, the "always be closing" approach to sales is the enemy of soulful persuasion. This may have worked in the past, but today's low-trust world demands an entirely different approach to persuasion. The basic presumption behind that infamous saying is that everything a person says or does in the course of persuading someone should be aimed purely at getting to yes. It's about aggressively pushing your audience to make the decision you want them to make, whether it's in their interest or not. It's about finding a way to close the deal at all costs.

This is short-term thinking at its crudest. It's manipulative—and it doesn't work. People don't want to be forced into a decision; they want to make up their minds for themselves, on their own terms, for their own reasons, and in their own time.

A pushy, fast-talking style simply confirms people's worst instincts about what's motivating you. It reminds them that, for you, the decision at hand is purely transactional, and that you'll likely say or do anything to get them to do what you want. This view of human nature was summed up beautifully by another of my personal idols, Bruce Springsteen, in his song "Badlands," where he sings:

> Poor man wanna be rich
> Rich man wanna be king
> And a king ain't satisfied
> Till he rules everything

"Badlands" is about people never being satisfied and always trying to take more and more and more. This is the kind of win-at-all-costs attitude that kills persuasion. In most persuasive interactions, people already know that you want something out of them. The only way to elevate the situation above the purely transactional is to demonstrate to them that you care about something more than your own immediate gain—more than being rich, being king, or ruling everything. So if you find yourself slipping into "always be closing" mode, you're absolutely headed in the wrong direction.

## Don't Be a Brand—Be a Human Being

At some point over the last couple of decades it became trendy for people to talk about themselves as brands. The concept may date back to 1997, when business magazine *Fast Company* ran a well-known article entitled "The Brand Called You."[1] Since then, a belief in the persuasive power of cultivating one's brand has hardened into conventional wisdom. Courses on "personal branding" have become business-school staples, but most people encounter the notion much earlier in their education.[2] College students are often taught that crafting a personal brand can help them land on their feet after graduation. And even high school seniors are advised to build personal "brand equity" to help win a spot at the college of their dreams.[3] The idea is that a carefully tailored perfect public image, and a consistent "brand voice" across all social media channels, can help a person sell themselves to the world.

But as someone who works with top brands every day, I find this whole line of thought antiquated. The notion of "personal branding" is based on a conception of brands that no longer ap-

plies. In this view, brands are highly manicured corporate identities strategically designed to do only one thing: turn a profit.
They are, in a word, transactional.

This isn't what a brand is anymore. In fact, most of today's
brands are doing their best to get away from this idea. Much of
the work Mekanism does is aimed at giving brands meaning and
real emotional resonance. Put differently, it's our job to make
brands seem more human and relatable. That's why we place
such a premium on great storytelling.

It's also why we ask clients to invest in projects that aren't
motivated by their bottom line. Through a formula we've developed, called "Make Good," Mekanism works with brands to
identify their core purpose—the reason they exist beyond turning a profit. From there, we help to identify a social good that
aligns with that purpose and find ways to advance that social
good that aren't purely self-serving for the brand. This helps
brands become more soulful.

What makes our work necessary is the fact that the old,
profit-driven, transactional model of brands leaves consumers
cold. According to a recent Meaningful Brands survey, Americans wouldn't care if three-quarters of the brands they use completely went away tomorrow.[4]

On the other hand, brands that demonstrate that they care
about more than just turning a profit are far better at resonating
with consumers. The 2018 Cone/Porter Novelli Purpose Study
found that 88 percent of Americans would buy a product from a
purpose-driven company. So three-quarters of Americans don't
care about the brands they use, but 88 percent want to buy from
brands that have a purpose. These numbers are too staggering to
ignore. That's why the modern brand has to provide a product

or service, turn a profit, *and* stand for something meaningful. Brands that have done this with huge success include our brand partner Ben & Jerry's, which uses ice cream to help fight racial injustice, promote fair trade, and get out the vote; Warby Parker, which launched their eyewear company with a "get a pair, give a pair" model; and of course Patagonia, which is a global force in helping protect the environment.

The objects of our emotional responses—and the things we naturally form relationships with—aren't corporate identities but other living, breathing human beings. Our work helps brands adopt many of the attributes of people, in part by giving them purpose and meaning that transcends simple profit. Marketing researchers call this phenomenon "brand anthropomorphism," which is essentially helping to personify brands. And there's a rich literature aimed at uncovering how brand anthropomorphism works its persuasive magic and what factors ultimately make brands seem more human.[5]

This raises an obvious question: If today's brands are so committed to becoming more like people, then why are individuals so eager to become old-fashioned brands? If anything, a persuasive personal character is one that avoids many of the features that turn people off about traditional branding—particularly their concern with maximizing profits and their obsession with outward appearance.

That was the insight behind a headline from the satirical publication *The Onion*: "'I Am a Brand,' Pathetic Man Says." The article describes this fictional person in passing as "a sad excuse for a man" and "hopeless."[6]

## A Tale of Two Brands

It's no wonder, then, that some of the biggest marketing missteps I've seen in recent years occurred when a company confirms the negative preconceptions surrounding brands. One of my favorite examples involves McDonald's "Create Your Taste" campaign from a few years ago. The idea was to allow customers to create customized burgers using an in-store touchscreen display. Customers could also submit their creations online so that the public could vote for their favorite burger.

When the campaign was rolled out in New Zealand, however, it quickly became a target of Internet trolls. Inappropriate submissions with names like "Pound My Behind Daddy" and "Thin Privilege" flooded the interwebs.[7]

Now, the sentiment behind the campaign was a good one. McDonald's was trying to show that it cared about the unique preferences of its customers and was willing to go the extra mile to give them some creative control over the menu. It wasn't their fault that a bunch of clowns hijacked the campaign. But when things got dicey, the brand did not respond like a human. Instead of acknowledging the incident, commenting, and maybe even poking a little fun at itself, as a human being would, McDonald's shuttered the site and pretended nothing had happened.

Compare that episode to a similar crowdsourcing mishap by another marquee brand: Walmart. Back in 2012, the company launched a campaign that promised to send recording artist Pitbull to do a live show at whichever Walmart location got the most likes on Facebook. Like the McDonald's effort, the campaign was an attempt to transcend cold transaction by engaging with their customers and doing something that wasn't just about maximizing profits. Once again, as if on cue, the trolls descended. Using the hashtag #ExilePitbull, two Internet pranksters launched a campaign to send the rapper to the most remote Walmart in the United States—on the island of Kodiak, Alaska, home to only 6,130 people.[8]

Walmart could have easily reacted as McDonald's did, cutting their losses and quietly shutting down the campaign—just another corporation playing it safe in order to protect their image. Instead, they rolled with it. Pitbull released a video announcing that he would, in fact, head to Kodiak, Alaska. Even though it was "due to someone who thinks he was playing a prank," he explained, "you gotta understand that I will go anywhere in the world for my fans."[9] Then, in a truly inspired move, he invited the person who orchestrated the #ExilePitbull push, *Boston Phoenix* writer David Thorpe, to join him on the trip, and even posted a picture of the two together.

By responding like a human being, Walmart managed to turn a potential blunder into a wave of positive publicity and goodwill and the campaign got way more coverage than if the incident never had happened. After all, it's hard to hear that story and not side with Walmart—a brand—over the actual guys who were trying to embarrass and bully the company.

## Don't Squander Your Humanity

For a brand, coming off as human takes a great deal of thought, effort, and luck. But you and I are already humans. And if your goal is to be persuasive, the last thing you should do is squander that advantage by packaging yourself as just another "brand."

People are more persuasive than brands. Consider Nielsen's

2015 Global Trust in Advertising Survey, which examined the kinds of advertising that consumers are most likely to trust. The most widely trusted format by far was recommendations from friends and family, which 83 percent of respondents said they trust at least most of the time. Two-thirds, meanwhile, say they tend to trust online comments from people they don't know. Brand sponsorships and brand emails, on the other hand, garnered far less trust.[10] Add it all up, and many people would rather trust a stranger than a brand.

No surprise there, since it's at least possible for human beings to act selflessly or sacrifice for the common good. We can be motivated by values and goals that transcend dollars and cents. We care about things like fairness, friendship, and loyalty. Of course, most persuasive interactions are, at their core, transactional—you want something from the other person. But the audience needs something else in order to be persuaded. They need to feel, intuitively, that the persuader cares about more than just getting a yes. Effective persuaders care about purpose. They are soulful.

## To Hell with Transactions

The old "always be closing" approach and the current concern with "personal branding" are both examples of a style of persuasion whose time has come and gone. Specifically, these strategies emphasize the transactional nature of persuasive interaction while downplaying or completely ignoring the kinds of human considerations that actually change minds and move people to action. The best alternative to such short-term persuasive techniques is one that is able to sacrifice opportunities for immediate gain in the service of the big picture—or, as I like to call it, *playing the long game.*

## Play the Long Game

Transactions are about getting what you want; the long game is about forging relationships. "Always be closing" is about pushing people to do something; the long game is about pulling people toward your way of seeing things by engaging them on a human level. And whereas the old transactional approach to sales practically announces to one's audience that they're being sold on something, the long game takes the emphasis off the decision at hand.

Perhaps the greatest practitioner of the long game I've ever met is the legendary talent manager Shep Gordon. This is the man behind some of the biggest acts in entertainment, including Alice Cooper, Blondie, Rick James, and Jimi Hendrix. He's also responsible for inventing the concept of the celebrity chef, repping people like Emeril Lagasse, Wolfgang Puck, and Daniel Boulud.[11] He is beloved by Hollywood, British royalty, and even the Dalai Lama.

What's amazing is that over the course of a half century in the entertainment and restaurant industries, Gordon built this roster of clients without ever signing formal contracts. His relationships are primarily based entirely on handshakes. Handshakes! As he explains it, he never liked bringing contracts into the mix, "because I didn't want that moment. I mean, if you don't feel I'm giving you value, if you think this is a one-sided relationship, go to someone else."[12] He was that confident in his ability and talent.

He practiced *compassionate business*—he calls it using "coupons." These were favors or loans that he would give out to his clients or friends during difficult times. When the legendary comedian Groucho Marx was struggling in his later years, Shep cashed in some of these "coupons" to revive Groucho's career.

This way of doing business lets the people he works with know from the start that he's interested not in the immediate transaction but the long-term relationship. And that dynamic is a major reason that the world's biggest stars trust him to look out for their interests. Sure, he's given up more than a few paydays. But if he was focused only on maximizing his own wealth, he never would have achieved the success—or the influence—that he has. I mean, Shep got to travel with the Dalai Lama. Talk about good karma.

One example of how Shep brilliantly built careers was when he brought Alice Cooper over from the United States to play Wembley Stadium. "It was a ten-thousand-seat show. We had only sold fifty tickets. So I thought, how do I get people in England to know and care who Alice Cooper is?"

Shep had built the musician's career by hitting on one simple truth: teenagers want to do anything their parents *don't* want them to do. So Shep came up with a quick and inexpensive plan. He printed a huge photo of Alice Cooper naked with a snake wrapped around him and pasted it on the side of a moving truck. He then paid the driver to make sure the truck broke down in Piccadilly Circus during rush hour, bringing traffic to a standstill. Shep also teased all the British tabloids to let them know that something important was about to happen in Piccadilly Circus and that they needed to cover it. So there in the middle of Piccadilly Circus during rush hour was this monster-sized billboard of a huge naked Alice Cooper with a snake wrapped around him, and with dozens of press outlets taking pictures, local news channels filming it, hundreds of cops, and a gaggle of trapped Londoners. Teenagers loved the stunt; adults hated it. Alice Cooper made all the tabloids and news coverage the next day—and the Wembley concert completely sold out in twenty-four hours. Plus the anti-parent anthem "School's Out" made it to number one in England. This type of energy, bravado, and fast thinking made Shep indispensable to his clients. And a handshake was all that was required.

The documentary film *Supermensch: The Legend of Shep Gordon* is devoted entirely to Shep and the style that made him so beloved by his clients. The title couldn't be more apt. *Mensch* is a Yiddish word that refers to a person of integrity and honor and directly translates to "human being."

Handshakes and the long-game approach even worked on me in my own business dealings. My friend Jon Bier runs the PR firm Jack Taylor. Over the years we've developed a relationship where we do favors for each other, connect clients to each other, kick around ideas, and generally look out for each other. A few months ago Jon came to me with a truly inspired—and slightly hard-to-believe—idea for a business venture. He and a partner, Brent Underwood, were planning on investing in an actual ghost town in California's Inyo Mountains, about two hundred miles north of Los Angeles.[13] The place, known as Cerro Gordo, is an authentic piece of the Wild West, complete with old-timey saloon and theater, and it was up for sale. Cerro Gordo, which means "fat hill," has twenty-two structures, including a church and abandoned hotel. In the late 1800s it was California's largest producer of silver. It is currently in a fairly run-down and untouched state and is believed to be haunted. Jon and Brent are planning on turning it into a vacation destination, full of modern amenities—but without destroying its historical character.

Jon and Brent wanted me to invest and be a part of it. Jon approached me and asked if I'd put my hard-earned money into an abandoned ghost town.

If it had been almost anybody else, I'd have been more than a little suspicious. Jon was, after all, trying to get me to be part owner of run-down buildings in the middle of nowhere. How much more like *Glengarry Glen Ross* can you get? But it wasn't just anybody making the pitch. Jon and I had established a rapport. He always gave advice freely and has never before tried to capitalize on that relationship. It was clear to me that he wouldn't have come to me if he didn't think I stood to gain from this project. So I wrote him a check—based on nothing more than the character he had established during the course of our relationship. Like Shep, a handshake was good enough for me. He had played the long game, and in this situation I was happy to reward him for it. And so were our other friends, including Ryan Holiday, Tero Isokauppila, Kelley Mooney, and some other trusting souls who can vouch for Jon and Brent.

## Selling Is Self-Defeating

One reason the long-game approach to influence is so effective is that it helps deal with one of the central paradoxes of persuasive communication: the fact that, when people think they're being persuaded, they're often less likely to be won over.

Consider a study by psychologists Elaine Walster and Leon Festinger from 1962. Their goal was to evaluate whether messages are more persuasive when the listener overhears them without the speaker's knowledge than if the speaker delivers the messages openly. To do this, they designed an experiment using students from an introductory psychology class at Stanford University.

Participants were divided up into groups and given a tour of the psych lab, apparently as part of their course. At some point during the tour, the participants were led into an observation room. This was a small area where students could see into a large room through a one-way mirror and listen in with headphones—the same setup as an interrogation room on a cop show.

On the other side of the one-way mirror were a few graduate students, just hanging out. As the tour guide explained, since the observation area isn't always in use, grad students often treat it as a lounge. The participants were then asked to practice their "blind listening" skills by listening in on the graduate students' conversation.

Here's where things get interesting. Some participants were led to believe that the graduate students on the other side of the glass *didn't* know they were being listened to. As far as these participants were concerned, they were eavesdropping on a private conversation. However, other participants were told that the graduate students they were hearing knew full well that there was an audience on the other side of the mirror.

In both cases, the graduate students proceeded to have a lengthy, detailed discussion explaining that smoking didn't actually cause lung cancer. Referencing a bunch of fictional scientific studies, they laid out a case for why smoking might even benefit people's health by helping them relax. This was total BS, of course, but the graduate students made what sounded like a reasonable argument.

Sure enough, participants who thought they were seren-dipitously overhearing the conversation were significantly more swayed by this fake argument than those who knew the gradu-ate students were performing for an audience. In other words, overhearing a message—seemingly by accident—proved more persuasive than being deliberately told something.

Walster and Festinger suggest one reason for this: When a message is openly stated, listeners might suspect that the speaker is trying to sway them and that he or she is acting from ulterior motives. When you hear something by accident, however, that thought doesn't even cross your mind.[14] As far as you know, the speaker had no idea you were listening. So how could that per-son be trying to persuade you?

This makes sense. If a salesperson tells me straight out that I should buy an iPhone and not an Android, one of the first things I think is, "What's in it for him?" When I overhear that person talking to his colleague behind the register about why Apple makes the superior phone, I'm sold. It doesn't occur to me that he's trying to influence me.

You are not going to hire actors to walk around town casu-ally endorsing your message in the hopes they'll be overheard. But giving people the hard sell is a fairly difficult way to change their beliefs—maybe the worst. People need to know they're making up their own minds about whether to trust you, whether your position is worth endorsing, or whether they should buy what you're selling. Allowing them to do so involves playing the long game.

## They Call Them "Influencers" for a Reason

The persuasive benefits of playing the long game can be seen in the recent adoption of what advertisers term "influencer marketing." This is an approach to selling that relies on the clout of social media celebrities—or "influencers," as they have come to be known.

People who garner enormous followings on platforms such as YouTube and Instagram have mainly done so by playing the long game. They have built trust with their followers by being open and honest about their values, interests, and character. Their fans, meanwhile, have come to know and love these individuals through daily exposure over the course of months or years. As Brendan Gahan, head of Mekanism's social media and influencer marketing division, Epic Signal, has written, "YouTubers, and vloggers in particular, are able to build a relationship with their fans that feels as close and intimate as a long and deep friendship for the viewer."[15]

So when a YouTube personality delivers a brand's message, it lends a degree of credibility and persuasiveness to that product that can only be achieved through the kind of long-term commitment that influencers have made to their fans. This is why one mention from the right social media influencer can crash an online retail website or send crowds of people to an event.

These individuals aren't brands, and most of them aren't in the business of making a quick sale. They are people who are skilled at forging real, human relationships. Playing the long game, in other words, means cultivating the same kind of trust, respect, and influence that have made these social media stars so persuasive.

## How to Play the Long Game

When it comes to achieving this kind of character, there are rules that you should observe in order to play the long game for deep and consistent payoffs.

### Rule 1: Never Sell Anything You Wouldn't Buy Yourself

The idea is simple enough: if you don't actually believe in the idea, product, vacation destination, restaurant, or concert that you're selling, then you shouldn't be selling it—end of story.

You might get away with being disingenuous now and again. But if you're regularly hawking things that you don't actually believe in—or even that you're just agnostic about—it will catch up with you pretty quickly. Over time, it will become obvious to others in myriad ways that you're not the kind of person who's worth trusting. And that's a reputation you will have absolutely earned.

The challenge here is that life is forever presenting us with attractive opportunities to violate this principle. There will always be times when it's convenient or potentially lucrative to take a position that you don't actually support. So it's critical that anytime you're aiming to change somebody's mind, ask yourself: "Do I think this person will be better off if they adopt my position? Or am I just trying to influence them so that I can enrich myself, make my life easier, avoid more work, or advance some other goal?"

The answer is usually pretty obvious, but not always. We are incredibly skilled at deceiving ourselves, never more so than when the truth gets in the way of our immediate desires. Taking a moment to be honest with yourself before you set out to persuade people makes it harder to indulge this impulse.

The process begins with a conscious decision to hold yourself accountable by refusing to persuade anybody to do anything that you wouldn't do yourself.

## Withering on the Vine: The High Price of Dishonest Persuasion

Some of my own biggest failures, which I've turned into learning opportunities, can be traced directly to my willingness to sell something I didn't believe in. One memorable example came a few years back when one of my colleagues had an idea for capitalizing on a much-hyped social media technology called Vine. For those of you who don't remember, Vine was a video platform owned by Twitter that allowed users to post six-second videos that would play in a loop. It was the snackable version of YouTube and a precursor to similar video efforts by Facebook and Instagram. And at the time it seemed like the next big thing.

As my colleague Andre Ricciardi saw it, one of the big problems with Vine was that there were real limitations to how you could view these videos. For instance, there was no way to organize or search for Vine loops. There were no dedicated channels and no single place where they were aggregated. His idea was to use Mekanism's resources to build what amounted to a Vine search engine, which we aptly named PEEKit. When he and a few of my other colleagues first came to me with the idea, they felt like this was a once-in-a-lifetime chance to make a lot of money. At that time Twitter was on a buying spree, purchasing companies like TweetDeck and Tweetie for small fortunes.[16]

All those technologies offered was a better way to organize and view tweets. If we could do the same thing for Vine loops, we reasoned, Twitter could make us rich too.

On top of that, if Vine took off, we would be able to bring clients into the fold, offering them prime placement on PEEKit's Vine channels. At the time, Mekanism had already made a name for itself as a leader in social media marketing, so this seemed like an obvious way to build on that reputation. The fact that Twitter had bought Vine from its creators before the service even launched only strengthened the case for it. If the tech billionaires in Silicon Valley were so keen on the product, there must be gold (not silver) in them thar hills, we thought. And so my partners and I agreed to go along.

But I never truly felt it in my gut. Honestly, I didn't understand why anyone would use Vine or why it was getting so much attention. And I definitely wasn't sure that people would have a need for a site that aggregated these super-short videos and made them searchable. I mean, Twitter was about free-flowing condensed thoughts and conversations. Poorly shot six-second video content was not the core of the Twitter experience.

After several months of intensive work by our production teams, along with a hefty financial investment, we got the site up and running. I touted it to clients and tried my best to explain why it was such an amazing opportunity for their brands.

Twitter shuttered Vine in January 2017, long after the initial buzz had subsided. As it turned out, a lot of people felt the same way as I did about Vine. And as Vine went, so went PEEKit.

This wasn't the first business I'd helped launch that didn't pan out. And there will be similar face-plants in my future—that's a risk you always run when you get behind any new venture. What bothered me most about this project in particular wasn't the time and money that were wasted building the platform and promoting it. No, it was the fact that I had tried to sell this product even though I didn't believe in it myself. I was pouncing on what I saw as an opportunity to make some fast money. I was thinking transactionally. Had I been playing the long game, I would have been honest with myself that I didn't believe in the venture, and kept my powder dry for opportunities that I could actually get behind.

## Rule 2: The Simple Power of No

In a way, this is the flip side of the previous principle. If you're only taking positions that you genuinely agree with, then you are going to have to say no to a ton of things. Conventional wisdom might tell you that if you're aiming to sway someone, you should say yes as much as humanly possible. But nobody trusts a yes-man—or a yes-woman. Why should they? If you routinely say things just to make people feel good about themselves, then you aren't a reliable source of information. On the other hand, if you're an authentic human being with passions, principles, and integrity—in short, a person of character—you're going to find yourself saying no. Similarly, if you're interested in the other person's long-term well-being and not just in getting what you want out of them, then you're going to have to tell them when you think they're making a mistake and not just let them make it. Sometimes that's what a relationship demands.

If I think a potential client's marketing strategy is ill-conceived or incoherent and I'm asked directly to give my opinion, I'm going to tell them that their brand needs some work and why. I'll do it in a way that's professional and that respects their opinion, particularly if I don't know the person very well. And you also can't be afraid to tell potential clients when you might not be the best company or person to handle a particular job. I've had clients come to me with very attractive offers that I've had to turn down because the timeline was too tight or we didn't have the right staff to make it happen. I could have told them "no problem," taken their money, and given them mediocre work. But odds are they'd never call us again.

Of course, things don't always go smoothly when you tell someone no. It's not a word people like to hear. And it's tempting to buckle under the pressure when exchanges get tense. These are the times when it's necessary to push back with force. If someone—a client, a colleague, a neighbor, anybody—is demanding something that my own sense of integrity prevents me from doing, I have no problem being a jerk about it. As long as it's for a good, positive reason, standing your ground and not being afraid of a little conflict isn't just acceptable, it's respect able. On the other hand, going against your principles and placating someone just for the sake of notching small wins will make you a lot less influential in the long term.

Being willing to say no when it matters is something you should do reflexively, without thinking. But from the standpoint of persuasion, this habit also has tactical benefits, at least if you're playing the long game. Passing up an opportunity for easy flattery or quick money reveals to the other person that you care about things other than making a lucrative deal or getting the answer you want. It makes you more trustworthy, and most of all, it makes you more human. There is no more powerful word in the English language than "no." This will help you get to the right work or job or opportunity when the time comes.

## How Martin Puris Used the Power of No to Make Advertising History

The power of no was driven home to me by one of my favorite figures from the history of advertising, Martin Puris. He's the man behind one of the most legendary taglines in the history of the business: BMW's "The Ultimate Driving Machine."

The tag has been in continuous use for over forty years—an unheard-of accomplishment. And it helped turn the brand from an obscure Bavarian carmaker into arguably the most iconic luxury auto brand in the United States. What I learned from my conversations with Martin, however, is that this advertising milestone would never have happened were it not for his own ability to say no when it mattered.

Puris first got a chance to pitch for BMW's business back in 1974, just a few months after he and his partners Ralph Ammirati and Julian AvRutick had founded the advertising agency Ammirati Puris AvRutick (later just A&P). Each of them had broken away from bigger agencies in the hopes of striking out on their own and doing the kind of subversive, holy-shit creative work that was transforming the advertising industry in that era.

At the beginning, nobody would have mistaken A&P for a polished Madison Avenue operation. Except for a single secretary, Ammirati Puris AvRutick wasn't just the name of the company; it was the company. And they operated out of a suite in New York's Delmonico Hotel.

As Puris tells it, those first few weeks were an exciting time. Unfortunately, the fledgling agency had yet to land a single new account since opening its doors, which was a problem, because in a matter of weeks the company would be flat broke, its principals forced to go back to work for somebody else. A&P was starting to look less like an up-and-coming creative agency and more like three guys killing time in a rented hotel room.

A&P's dearth of business in these early months wasn't entirely an accident. In fact, it was a little bit by design. The standard route to building a client roster didn't appeal to A&P's founders, and especially not to Ammirati. As he once put it, "Begin with a lot of little cats and dogs and you spend the rest of your life trying to upgrade." That's not how A&P would do things. They were in this game to do outstanding work for prestige clients. Cobbling together a bunch of mom-and-pop accounts might keep the lights on, but it would make it harder to land the kind of business they were after: "No decent blue-chip account wants that kind of agency, and we wanted blue-chip accounts." So they turned down a lot of work early on, and put their faith in the power of no to catapult them to the big leagues.

It was only by chance that they caught wind of a German car company named BMW that was just getting serious about breaking into the American market. Puris made contact through an old friend at Young & Rubicam, and before long A&P was in the running for the business. The account, however, was hardly theirs for the taking. Two other agencies—the orders-of-magnitude-larger Benton & Bowles and Ted Bates—were also given a shot. Both agencies had decades of experience working with top-tier brands, from Budweiser to M&M's and Colgate toothpaste.

Moreover, Puris soon realized that introducing BMW to the American market would be no easy task. The automaker was positioning themselves as a luxury brand, but their cars were nothing close to what American consumers expected from a luxury vehicle. The early 1970s was the heyday of the pimpmobile—gaudy large rectangles of sheet metal, chrome, and vinyl. They were larded with unnecessary features like power-adjustable seats, Cartier clocks in the dash, and wood paneling. If you paid a lot of money, you expected a lot of car in return, as well as a healthy choice of color schemes. The BMW 2002, meanwhile, was a compact sedan that reminded many of the Chevy Corvair—a car that no American associated with luxury. Nevertheless, it carried a price tag that rivaled a Cadillac's.

It was during a trip to Munich, while talking to one of BMW's engineers, that Puris had his first big insight into the brand's identity and how to present it to America. BMW was about substance over style. It was the car that engineers would build if they didn't have to answer to anybody, if they could throw out the rule book written by the stodgy establishment. It was a car for people who evaluated cars by how well they perform, not what they look like.

Puris also understood exactly what kind of American such a car would appeal to—people like him. He was among the first to realize that there was a large and growing group of people like himself who combined a distinctly 1960s countercultural passion with a drive for professional—and most definitely financial—success. If anybody could embrace this notion of "excellence for its own sake" that BMW's cars embodied, it was well-off baby boomers.

What's more, it was obvious to Puris that the luxury cars that so impressed his parents' generation left people like him cold. There was no Lincoln Continental for well-off young people. BMW could be that car.

He had his insight. Now he needed to execute, and that meant crafting a perfect tagline. His first instinct was to be witty, with lines like "Our status symbol is under the hood, not on it." But he knew this wasn't right. The line got the idea across, but with a smirk. It congratulated itself on its own cleverness.

He kept tossing lines at the wall to see what would stick. One stood out: "The ultimate driving machine vs. the ultimate sitting machine." Again, he thought, too much wordplay. Lines like that might work well in one-off ads—as many of his discarded ideas eventually did. But the tagline had to announce BMW's identity in indisputable terms. Nevertheless, there was something in this last line that rang true. Like so many great creative accomplishments, a lot comes down to thoughtful editing. And as Puris looked at the line, he saw what needed to happen. Forget comparisons and skillful turns of phrase, he thought. Keep it dead simple. There's only one thing consumers needed to know about this car, and he could say it four words: "The Ultimate Driving Machine." Yes. This was the Ultimate Driving Machine. The money all went under the hood, not to the bells and whistles in the cockpit.

With that tagline, Puris knew he had it. His partners, however, weren't so sure. It was too simple, they complained, too cold and utilitarian. It didn't even sound like a tagline. Plus nobody thinks about luxury when they hear the word "machine." These were all reasonable criticisms—especially when you consider that A&P's entire existence depended on this one pitch. It was no time to experiment.

Here again is where the power of no proved absolutely critical. Puris disagreed with his colleagues and refused to budge. They had started the business to do great, pathbreaking work. And if they were going to go bust, they might as well do it with something truly original. So A&P headed to Munich to pitch BMW, ready to stake their entire business on four words that only Puris truly believed would sell.

Puris told me that the moment he revealed "The Ultimate Driving Machine" during his pitch, it was obvious they had won the business. The three executives in the room immediately turned to each other and began to discuss the idea quietly, nodding and smiling the entire time.

But even though the client was thoroughly sold, they weren't thrilled about A&P's bench strength, their stability, and, most important, their asking price. What followed was a month of haggling. BMW wanted to just buy the line and work with another agency.

Once again, Puris leaned on the power of no. He insisted that it was all or nothing. "They kept saying, 'It's too expensive'; we kept saying, 'Well, this isn't an offer. That's what it's going to cost,'" Puris said. By this time it was already late 1974, and the agency had exactly enough resources to last them three to four more weeks. "They know by this time that we don't really have any other clients," Puris told me. "We're just like Daffy Duck, right?" It was the very definition of a weak negotiating position.

But the three partners had no intention of dropping their rate or just giving up their line. For one, they knew that the man who would ultimately make this decision, BMW's head of marketing, Bob Lutz, loved the idea. "He was the most effusive in the meeting," Puris remembers. It took balls, but their answer remained the same: "If you don't want to do it, just don't do it." As Puris later heard it, Lutz told his marketing team that "they're either the smartest guys in the world, or the dumbest fucking guys in the world. We're not going to know which they are until after we hire them. So just fucking hire 'em."

A&P had landed BMW with only ten days of cash left. With billings of $900,000 a year (which was a good amount at the time), the account was enough to pay off their bills and invest in hires.

In the scheme of things, the success of a small advertising agency isn't world-changing. But Puris's story still demonstrates the power of no to turn one's convictions into a reality. He said no to making a bunch of quick sales to small clients to keep the agency afloat early on. He said no to his colleagues when they asked him to write a safer tagline for BMW. And he said no when the carmaker demanded they lower their rate and thus compromise their creative vision. In each instance, Puris was revealing that both he and his fledgling agency cared about something more than just turning a profit. And those decisions added up to enormous influence, both in that pitch to BMW and in Puris's career in the years that followed.

## Rule 3: Never Let Relationships Drop to Zero

Truly persuasive people care more about relationships than transactions. It should come as no surprise, then, that the habit of forging, maintaining, and valuing relationships for their own sake is central to developing a persuasive character.

The person who only comes knocking when he needs something from you isn't in a good position to be persuasive. And the reason he isn't is that he clearly doesn't give a shit about you. He doesn't have a relationship with you, and he doesn't want one. But go out of your way to nurture your relationships, and the persuasive benefits will follow on their own.

In my experience, the most common relationship-killer is simple neglect. Taking steps to ensure that none of your relationships drop to zero—that you never lose contact with anyone for too long—is half the battle when it comes to keeping relationships alive. Here are a few techniques I use to make staying in touch a little more automatic.

## Set a Reminder

Set a repeating reminder to check in with the person, usually quarterly. It all depends on who the person is and what kind of relationship you have. But if they're important enough to have in your contacts, then they're important enough to stay in touch with.

## Connect with Four

Pick four people a week to touch base with. It doesn't need to be a long email or phone conversation—it could just be a quick "I was thinking about X and that reminded me of you" text message. It could also be a face-to-face meeting or scheduled phone call.

I make sure that I have regular one-on-ones with everyone in my company. This chews up a lot of time, but it gives everyone a chance to share their unique insights with the CEO and let me know what they need to be successful or what ideas they have for making the company better. This habit enables me to build real relationships with each and every employee in the company, and for that, it's a great investment in time.

## Shift from Social to Personal

Next time you go to share a thought on social media—whether you're tweeting out praise for a new TV show or liking an article on Facebook—don't. Instead, go through your contacts and figure out who specifically would appreciate the recommendation or insight. Then send out a few emails or text messages aimed at individual people. In other words, use your thought to restart a personal conversation.

## Bring People Together

Look for opportunities to introduce people. Have a client who loves classic guitars? Introduce him to your high-school friend who restores old Les Pauls. Is your neighbor considering going to law school? Put her in touch with your cousin who teaches torts at NYU Law School. Don't force the interaction; just make the introduction and let them do the rest. Your goal is to value relationships for their own sake—and that includes other people's relationships.

## Treat "No" as "No . . . for Now"

Another way to put relationships before transactions is to treat persuasive interactions not as endings or "moments of truth" but as beginnings, or as episodes within a larger relationship.

For instance, if a client I'm pitching turns me down, I think of that answer not as a "no" but as a "no . . . for now." I do this even if there's no obvious opportunity to change the client's mind in the near future. Why? Because I intend to keep in touch with this person and will likely encounter them again. When

I do, that no will be but one event in the course of our relationship. That relationship could lead to new and better things
in the future. Or it might not. But the pitch isn't the end of a
relationship.

One benefit of this shift in thinking is that it takes some pressure off the pitch itself and makes me more confident, more re-
laxed, and less desperate in my interactions with the person I'm
pitching. This, in turn, helps the client not to feel like he or she
is being forced into a decision by some sweaty salesman. It takes
the emphasis off of the transaction and places it on the relationship, even if the difference is purely subconscious. The habitual
tendency to frame situations in this way without thinking is a
hallmark of a persuasive character.

Over the course of my career this general outlook has served
me well. In fact, I can say with certainty that had we not learned
to value relationships above transactions in precisely this way,
Mekanism wouldn't have one of its biggest current clients, the
financial services firm Charles Schwab.

We've been working with the brand for more than five years.
But when we initially sought their business, they didn't even let
us in the door for an official pitch. Instead of treating their reaction as a firm "no," however, we took it as a "no . . . for now."
Over the next few years our team made a point to maintain our
relationship with our contacts there.

We made sure they got our quarterly company emails announcing awards and achievements—not just to brag, but to
make them an unofficial member of our agency's community.
Most of all, we made sure to ask for nothing in return. We were
maintaining our relationship and giving the company some
sense of the way we do business and the work we do for other
clients, not selling. At New Year's we sent them branded gifts

from us. We stayed in contact and remembered to never let our relationship drop to zero.

Eventually we got a small project, which we treated like the most important work of our career. That project turned into another project. And sure enough, when Charles Schwab found themselves in the market for a new agency, we were immediate contenders, and we won. This happened in large part because we kept in touch and showed that we cared about the relationship. If all we'd wanted was a signed contract, then keeping in touch over the course of years wouldn't have been a very efficient way of going about it. We were in it for the long haul, though, and we are their agency today because of it.

## Rule 4: Put Some Skin in the Game

Of course, forging a long-term relationship isn't always enough. And there will be plenty of times when you'll find yourself having to persuade someone you've just met. In these instances, you need to look for other ways to establish yourself as someone who cares about the other person's long-term interests and not just your own immediate gain. One strategy is to put some of your own skin in the game. How do you do that? By taking on some of the risks involved in whatever decision is at hand.

Some of the most effective advertising relies on precisely this principle. A recent study by researchers at Northwestern's Kellogg School of Management looked at which kinds of advertisement messages were judged most effective by consumers. At the top of that list were ads that included money-back guarantees and those that promised to match a competitor's best price for a particular product.[17] Now, this isn't exactly the kind of advertisement that Mekanism trades in. But the findings hit home.

In both of these examples, the seller is demonstrating that the interests of the consumer are more important than either closing a sale or wringing the most money out of the transaction. They are, in other words, investing in a long-term relationship at the expense of short-term gain. Incidentally, some of the least trustworthy messages, according to the Kellogg School study, were those that forced consumers to decide quickly by leveraging a limited-time offer—a classic case of the kind of hard sell that is always best to avoid.

If you're trying to persuade a new friend to go to a Japanese restaurant instead of a Mexican joint, you might offer to pick up the whole tab and take them to the Mexican place next time if they're disappointed in the rainbow roll you've been craving. This approach doesn't just minimize the risks for the other person; it demonstrates to them that you care about their satisfaction, not just your own, and that you're willing to deal with the consequences if they're not happy with their decision.

If you don't genuinely think that the other person will enjoy the sushi, then you shouldn't be trying to change their mind in the first place. But putting some skin in the game is a great way to make this aspect of your character even more obvious.

 **RECAP**

It's a strange irony that some of the best-known advice about selling actually undermines the most powerful persuasive tool we possess—our humanity.

Whether it's the current obsession with "personal branding" or the old-school mantra "always be closing," these techniques seem to reduce persuasion to the purely transactional. In that view, persuasion is nothing more than a slick way of saying "Give me what I want." Aside from being pretty unseemly, this whole outlook is also ineffective. People don't like being sold things, and they'd rather deal with a human being over a brand.

Relationships over transactions. It's always better to play the long game. The four rules:

1. Never sell anything you wouldn't buy yourself.
2. Don't be afraid to say no.
3. Never let relationships drop to zero.
4. Put some skin in the game.

When I find myself lapsing into "always be closing" mode and going for the hard sell, it's usually because I failed to abide by one or more of the above tenets. Ideally, these core rules will become close to second nature. But until that happens, adhering to them will take effort and focus.

When you persuade by playing the long game, you'll never just be closing.

# PRINCIPLE 1: ORIGINAL

Being your real, original self in every interaction is a must for soulful persuasion. Most people can recognize phoniness instinctively. If you're hiding your true intentions, failing to resonate on a human level, or engaging in purely transactional thinking, it shows through, no matter how hard you try.

There are three habits that, when taken together, can combat this kind of artificiality and let your audience know that you're coming from someplace real and personal—someplace authentically you.

### Be Yourself—Everyone Else Is Taken

From time to time, we all feel tempted to be the kind of person others want us to be. This is especially true in high-stakes interactions in which personal impressions matter. But it's always a mistake.

Your goal should be to abandon your concerns about how others are perceiving you and speak from your smart gut. Don't be afraid of wearing your personal idiosyncrasies and passions on your sleeve. Collect role models and draw inspiration from their uniqueness. And stick to your core values.

### Learn to Be a Great Storyteller

Fact, argument, and reason might speak to the intellect, but to truly engage you will also need storytelling. If you want to make your point of view real to an audience—especially a skeptical audience—you need to be able to transport them emotionally through narrative.

Fortunately, storytelling is a skill like any other, which means that, with enough concerted practice, it can be learned. Collect original stories that are especially meaningful to you and that convey ideas you find important. Keep an eye out for storytellers that you are drawn to and dissect what makes them so good. And remember that familiar tales are often the most powerful.

### Never Be Closing

Being real means resisting the urge to go for the quick close or to package yourself as an old-fashioned brand. Today's best brands try hard to avoid the perception that they are purely transactional entities. They want to be more human.

Demonstrate that you care about things other than just making money or getting what you want as quickly as possible. Don't sell anything you wouldn't buy yourself—whether it's a product, a service, or an idea. Don't be afraid to say no, even if it costs you something in the short term. Care about your relationships, and do your best to see that none of them ever drops to zero. And show that you're genuinely committed to whatever you're advocating by putting your own skin in the game. Let go of short-term transactional thinking and start playing the long game.

PRINCIPLE 2

# GENEROUS

We
a l l
know peo-
ple we would
describe as naturally
generous. It's a character
trait that runs deep, and it's evident in a host of little ways. Like the
other traits discussed in this book, generosity is an attribute that is good in and of itself. Generous people are the sorts of individuals we enjoy doing
favors for. When they succeed, we are truly happy for them.
And when they walk into a room, we're always glad to
see them. We want to help them be successful at
every turn. And, most important, when they
express a view or advocate a course
of action, we genuinely want to
agree with them. That's
why, when you end up
giving, you end
up getting.

Chapter 4

# give yourself away

---

*They who give have all things.*
*They who withhold have nothing.*

—Hindu proverb

We're often told that if you want something from another
person, it helps if you grease the wheels by giving him or her
something first—a classic tit-for-tat exchange. The effectiveness
of this strategy has been repeatedly confirmed by the clever experiments of academic researchers. But you don't have to consult
a psychology journal to see this idea in action. It's the reason why
food and beverage makers offer free samples at Whole Foods
and drug companies shower doctors with free samples, branded
pens, and coffee mugs. It's why Netflix and Spotify give you a
free trial before they ask for money, and it's often why wealthy

businesspeople donate to political campaigns (and why politicians do favors for potential donors).

In his classic book on the science of persuasion, *Influence*, psychologist Robert Cialdini identifies this rule—which he dubs "the rule of reciprocation"—as "one of the most potent of the weapons of influence" available to us.[1] For instance, Cialdini cites one study in which restaurant servers who gave diners a free mint at the end of their meal saw their tips increase by 3 percent. Those who gave two mints—and mentioned to the diners that they were only supposed to give one—experienced a 14 percent tip increase.[2] The basic lesson in this study is clear: if you want something, you have to give something.

However, my approach to persuasion isn't about collecting "weapons of influence." It's about developing the character traits that compel people to take your side, not because of some tactical maneuver you've successfully executed but because of who you actually are.

With this in mind, we should aim to modify the lesson from Cialdini's rule of reciprocity: If you want to be persuasive, don't look for chances to engage in tit-for-tat exchanges. Be the kind of person who naturally thinks about giving things away. Attempt to leave every person you encounter with something valuable that they didn't have before they interacted with you—a useful piece of information, some helpful advice, a gift that advances them, anything that might be valuable for them.

In a word, be *generous*.

Unlike someone who has weaponized the rule of reciprocity in order to get a quick yes, a generous person gives habitually, without thinking, and without expecting anything in return. They see the world in terms of other people's needs, and they naturally identify ways of helping. The sociologist Christian

Smith defines generosity as "the virtue of giving good things to others freely and abundantly."[3] It's the opposite of selfishness and greed—even though this may end up benefiting you in the long run.

In fact, it's a great irony that when you give without regard for self-interest, you end up getting a lot in return. It's also an idea that is central to many ancient philosophies and religions.

A Chinese proverb tells us, "One who constantly gives will constantly have wealth and honor."

The New Testament teaches, "It is more blessed to give than to receive."[4]

And the Buddha believed, "Giving brings happiness at every stage of its expression."[5]

The latest scientific research has taken a while to catch up with this ancient wisdom, but it tends to agree. Generosity has been linked to greater levels of personal happiness, lower stress levels, better health, and longer life expectancy.[6]

But it also has significant benefits in the domain of persuasion.

## Giving Makes Us Human

Human beings have a natural capacity to give selflessly—at least in certain situations. But until recently, science saw this innate tendency as a mystery. Specifically, our willingness to be generous with people we may never meet again has stumped researchers in disciplines ranging from economics and game theory to evolutionary psychology. Why, for instance, do we feel compelled to tip restaurant servers when we're on vacation in a city we'll never visit again? If a stranger in the street asks you to help jump-start his car, why do we feel the need to help him out?

From an evolutionary perspective, there's no reason humans should have developed this willingness to sacrifice for strangers, since there's little chance that person will ever be in a position to either return the favor or bad-mouth us to our friends if we don't help. If we're designed by evolution to look out for ourselves and our kin, this feature of our psychology shouldn't be so universal. Nice guys are supposed to finish last, after all. And according to the brutal logic of natural selection, species that finish last don't stick around for very long. Yet in study after study, humans have shown themselves surprisingly willing to act altruistically toward anonymous people they are unlikely to meet again.

It was in 2011 that a group of scientists at the University of California, Santa Barbara, finally cracked this puzzle. The study—which was coauthored by, among others, Leda Cosmides and John Tooby, the founders of evolutionary psychology—used a series of computer models to test how this feature might have evolved in *Homo sapiens*. This enabled them to do something that couldn't be done with flesh-and-blood humans in a laboratory: simulate how our decision-making abilities took shape over thousands of generations.

The simulation began with five hundred virtual people, who were paired off for a classic situation from game theory known as the *prisoner's dilemma*. In that scenario, two partners—A and B—are arrested for a crime and held in separate prison cells. They face a choice: Do they roll over on their partner, or do they stay quiet? Under the rules of the game, if one of them defects and the other stays silent, the defector goes free and the other guy gets three years in the big house. If both stay silent, they'll each get a one-year prison sentence. And if they both defect, they'll each get two years behind bars. So the sentences range from one to three years based on the choice the player makes.

Because of how the rules of the game are written, it's always rational to defect—provided the game isn't repeated. If it is repeated, then there are significant costs to defecting and significant benefits from working together. If I roll over on my partner in round one and the game is repeated, then he's going to get me back by screwing me over in the next round. If I believe that the game is a onetime-only interaction, however, I have far less reason to look out for my partner in crime. In this way, the game mirrored the situation we face when deciding to tip a waiter in a foreign city. If I will never see that person again, it's rational to stiff him on a tip.

But the researchers included a critical feature in their computer simulation. Specifically, they built their model such that the virtual people didn't know whether each prisoner's dilemma situation would be a onetime deal (like the restaurant server in another city) or a repeated encounter. They had to figure that detail out using a bunch of not-completely-reliable cues from their environment and then decide whether or not to stay silent or to defect. Again, this was all modeled in a computer program so that the researchers could see which decision-making behaviors would stand the test of time over the course of ten thousand generations.

What they found was that the very same forces and circumstances that lead us to engage in tit-for-tat exchanges also result in a proclivity for generosity toward strangers. In a world where people tend to return favors, in other words, people who do favors without expecting anything in return—even when it's not entirely rational—are better off in the long run.

The reason for this is actually pretty simple: When you interact with a new person, you can never be sure whether or not you'll encounter him or her again. You can probably guess with some degree of confidence. But if you assume wrongly you'll never cross paths with someone again, your mistake can cost you dearly. Better to be generous just in case than to piss off someone who might be able to get you back. And so, the authors of the study conclude that "generosity, far from being a thin veneer of cultural conditioning atop a Machiavellian core, may turn out to be a bedrock feature of human nature."[7] So the reason it pays to be generous may have less to do just with the karma of Eastern philosophy and more to do with plain old game theory.

And not only is generosity a valuable tool for inspiring trust and getting people to cooperate with you, but it might even beat out the old tit-for-tat alternative that persuasion experts have been championing for years.

What is strange is that it took scientists so long to realize this fact.

## The Perks of Habitual Generosity

"You scratch my back, I'll scratch yours" has real limitations. For one, it doesn't inspire much trust. Each person is simply doing what's in his or her best interest. And if a better deal comes along, or the other person's needs change, the whole arrangement could break down in a hurry. This approach is really just a few notches above Cold War–era realpolitik—which doesn't exactly warm the heart.

In decades following World War II, the only thing preventing all-out war between the United States and the Soviet Union was the recognition that if either country attacked the other, the targeted country would retaliate, and the result would be total nuclear annihilation of both sides—so-called mutually assured destruction. There was no persuasion involved, beyond threats.

Needless to say, this is not a sound strategy for forging agreement, as evidenced by the number of times a minor misunderstanding between the United States and the Soviet Union nearly resulted in nuclear apocalypse. Consider what happened in November 1979, when the computers at an American nuclear warning center in Colorado detected what looked like a full-scale attack from the Soviets. The computers were showing that nuclear missiles were on their way to American nuclear facilities and other strategic locations around the country, including the Pentagon and the Alternate National Military Command Center. Soon U.S. nuclear bomber crews were sent to their planes, ten interceptor jets were put into the sky, missile operators were standing on high alert, and the president's "doomsday plane" left the ground in preparation for the worst. We were suiting up for a nuclear war that wouldn't end well for either country— or anybody on the planet, for that matter.

It was a false alarm. Someone at the North American Aerospace Defense Command (NORAD) had inserted a highly believable training program into the computer—either by accident or as the most reckless practical joke in the history of humanity.[8] When agreements are based purely on reciprocity and tit-for-tat arrangements, even a minor misstep can potentially blow up the whole thing (sometimes even the whole damn world).

The same is true when persuasion is built solely on the expectation of mutual benefit. If someone is only helping you because they expect you to return the favor, that alliance is inherently shaky. There's no basis for trust in these situations because they are purely transactional.

But we are willing to take a chance on a naturally generous person, we are happy when things go well for them, and we feel good about doing business with them. And we give them the benefit of the doubt if they don't come through from time to time, as we know their heart is in the right place—instead of getting our fighter jets in the air as quickly as possible and targeting our missiles on them.

As the UC Santa Barbara study shows, generosity also helps overcome a major problem facing the tit-for-tat approach—namely, that you can never be sure who will be in a position to do you a favor in the future. If you only give to those you believe can help you, you'll be much worse off in the long run than someone who is generous as a matter of course.

Evolution has built us to be generous by default, on the off chance that the stranger in need of a jump-start today turns out to be the person interviewing you for a job tomorrow. By being habitually generous, you set yourself up to benefit from those happy accidents whenever they do occur. These small, occasional wins can add up over time, like compound interest.

The tendency to be generous was embedded in all of us over the course of millions of years of evolution. Nevertheless, like any character trait, some people possess generosity in spades, while others . . . well, not so much. Regardless of which camp you fall into, each of us can learn through practice to be habitually generous.

For me, however, the process of becoming more generous starts with one simple rule.

## How to Be Generous:
## Give Something Away in Every Interaction

As the philosopher Christian B. Miller has written, for an act to be an instance of true generosity, a "person's motives in donating have to be primarily altruistic, or concerned with the well-being of those who would be helped, regardless of whether the donor will benefit in the process."[9] The person who only comes around when they need something from you is, by nature, a shitty persuader. People like that suck the life out of us. When their name appears in our inbox, our day automatically gets a little more meh and we roll our eyes. And when they tap on our office door, we immediately think, "Jesus, what does this dude want now?" That person is going to have a hard time winning you over under the best of circumstances.

On the other hand, an individual who leaves you just slightly better off every time you encounter him or her is precisely the person who is likely to get your attention when they come to you with a proposition, need a favor, or want to change your mind about something. How do you become this type of person? Simple. Every time you interact with someone—whether it's at a business meeting or at a family gathering, at a ball game or on a dinner date—try to give something away. Treat all of your encounters as a chance to be generous.

If you commit to doing this, you'll find that generosity comes in many forms. You can be generous with money and always pay the bill, but money is actually the least meaningful thing you can give away. If you go into every encounter thinking, "What can I contribute? How can I give away something valuable?," the answer usually falls into a few basic categories.

## Time, Attention, and Patience

I'm a busy guy. I run a company with offices in four cities servicing dozens of clients at any given time. I also have a great family and supportive friends. And on top of that, I love to work out, travel, play music from time to time, occasionally hang out with friends, read books (and sometimes foolishly attempt to write them), and learn new skills. I'm a hard-core doer. And for all of these reasons, I'm almost always strapped for time. There aren't enough hours in the day.

This makes time one of the most valuable assets I have. And not just any time, but the kind of time that comes with attention and genuine patience. For me, being generous with my time means that whenever someone I know asks for some of it, my default answer is going to be yes.

For instance, if someone wants me to sit in on a meeting or on a phone call at work, my answer is yes—even if it requires me to move things around on my schedule. If my presence and attention can help in even the smallest way, I want to be there. If a family member, friend, or colleague needs a sympathetic listener, I try to be all ears. And if a coworker or friend screws up and wants to explain what happened, I let them have their say and then form my opinion.

I don't always nail this. Sometimes I just don't have the time to give on that specific day or week. But if it's even remotely possible for me to give my time to improve someone else's circumstance, then I try to do it.

Not long ago my first instinct when someone asked me to give even a little of my time was to find a way to say no and get out of it—usually by explaining how busy I am. What I realized is that most of the people in my life already know how busy I am, which means they probably wouldn't be asking for my time if it wasn't important to them.

And by investing your valuable time in other people, they are much more willing to invest in you.

## Advice, Recommendations, and Information

Have you just listened to an amazing new album nobody is talking about? Or found a great out-of-the-way restaurant that blew your mind? Maybe you read an article or book that was transformational. Maybe you had an amazing insight about work, or learned a lesson about parenting the hard way.

If so, then don't keep these revelations to yourself. Rather, write them down in a notebook. Then think carefully about who in your life would benefit from that information. Finally, reach out to the person or people who came to mind. Rather than hoarding discoveries that have helped you, remember that wisdom is meant to be shared. And people love to be on other people's minds. It just makes them feel good.

## Compliments and Recognition

This might seem obvious, but it's easy to forget to praise others, especially if you yourself are feeling stressed or are just having a tough day. The truth is, noticing something positive about another person and expressing your appreciation honestly can change that person's day. I have to consciously work on this one. When you think of something positive, don't hold it in, say it.

On this front, it helps to make your compliments as specific as possible. Instead of telling a coworker, "Thanks for the hard work," tell her, "I know you've been busting your ass these last few weeks on project X. I wanted to let you know how much I appreciate it because your work is having a positive outcome for the company"—and then go on to explain exactly what the positive outcome is.

Similarly, if you experience success of any kind—whether professional or personal—think about who else played a role in achieving that victory. Odds are you didn't do it alone. So make sure to spread the credit around. Reach out to whoever contributed, share in the good news, and express your appreciation.

Maybe it's just saying, "Hey, that research you did really put us over the top in the pitch meeting yesterday." If your kid got into a great college, let his or her teacher know that the extra SAT prep they provided really made a difference. And let your significant other know that the hours he or she spent doing that extra thing for you both really paid off. Just make sure to be honest and specific about why.

By the same token, when things go wrong, resist the urge to assign blame to just a single individual. You have to acknowledge what went wrong, but try to do it in an honest, clear, but also kind manner.

Being generous in defeat is just as important as being generous in victory.

## Stuff

Then there are times when expressing your generosity calls for actual, physical stuff. I'm talking here about gifts. Gift-giving is an art form, no doubt about it. It can also be a chore. Who among us hasn't been caught unprepared the day before Valentine's Day, an anniversary, or a friend's birthday, frantically searching online, weighing the pros and cons of a scented candle, a bathrobe, or some other generic gift? It is very hard to keep up with all the dates and all the people you would want to celebrate. I never nail the dates. One way I've found to avoid this sad state of affairs is to be in gift-giving mode all year round—not specifically around official, legally designated gift-giving occasions.

What does that entail? For one thing, if I purchase something for myself that I'm super excited about or just find really useful, I make sure to buy another—or sometimes two more, if it's not insanely expensive. Could be a phone case, a tie clip, or the perfect space pen. Most often it's a book (when I find a book I love, I tend to buy multiple copies). Usually I have no idea whom I'll end up giving it to, which is part of the fun. This gift could sit in a drawer for months until I think of someone who would truly appreciate it or needs it at the time. But when the right occasion arises, I've got a thoughtful gift ready to go.

In this way, I make sure that when I find something I love, I'm also treating someone else I love.

## The Million-Dollar Hoodie

My agency prides itself on coming up with cool gifts to send out to our network: friends, family, and clients. Sure, a lot of companies have swag, but we try to make ours just a little bit different. For example, one year we designed a Mekanism hoodie that had the company name silkscreened in the same typeface as the Metallica logo. One year we chose a custom-designed box of cereal with hidden toy surprises inside. Another year we sent out a hollowed-out fake inspirational book with a branded corkscrew hidden inside. We want to get people wearing the brand or keeping the brand on their desks or offices.

In fact, it was a hooded sweatshirt that helped us land one of

our oldest clients, Ben & Jerry's ice cream. I had met a represen-
tative of the brand, Jay Curley, at a conference I attended, and
we got to talking. I'm a huge Ben & Jerry's lover, so I was just
happy to meet someone from the organization and exchange information. I immediately added him to our agency's mailing list
for free stuff like newsletters, conference invites, articles—and,
of course, our Mekanism hoodies.

As luck might have it, about ten months later Jay called to say
that Ben & Jerry's was in the market for a new agency. He probably wouldn't have remembered our agency were it not for the
fact that, he told me, he loved our Mekanism hoodie and wore
it. We were invited to pitch the business, which we ultimately
won. At the time of this writing, we've been their agency for
six years. That twenty-something-dollar sweatshirt rewarded
us with a great client and millions and millions of dollars in
revenue.

Was I trying to land a bank shot that turned a free hoodie
into a major company success? Nah. I was just trying to give
cool merchandise away to a cool person that I met. And as it
turns out, putting awesome stuff out into the world is a habit
that pays unexpected dividends.

## A Crash Course in Generosity

I've detailed some of the most common things you'll find yourself in a position to give—time, advice, compliments, gifts. But
making generosity a natural component of your character will
take practice. That process breaks down into three strategic
practices you can implement.

## Identifying the Need State

Go into key interactions thinking about what, if anything, you can contribute or what's being asked of you. Is this an opportunity to offer a useful piece of information? Or does the situation call for a bit of honest feedback? It could be that the person you've connected with would appreciate a copy of a book you just read. Don't feel the need to know ahead of time what the right response will be in each instance; once you begin seeing interactions as opportunities to give stuff away, the answer usually comes into focus. Go with your gut here.

## Automatic Yes

If you start understanding interactions in these terms, it will slowly become obvious what of value you are most willing to offer freely, and which things you are less eager to part with. Some people don't like sharing experiences from their personal life. Others are stingy with their time or attention. And some people can't bring themselves to give compliments. Make a note of which acts of generosity you instinctively say no to in your head, and then commit to turning most of those automatic nos into automatic yeses.

## Follow Up

Whenever possible, ensure that your act of generosity isn't an isolated incident. If I send a copy of one of my favorite books to somebody, I also shoot them a follow-up email to make sure they got it, share my thoughts on the book, and explain why I thought they'd appreciate it. With any luck, I turn that gift into a substantive conversation. This isn't always possible, of course. But in situations when it is, following up is a great way to extend a single act of generosity into something deeper and more rewarding.

 ## RECAP

It's long been thought that one of the best ways to wield influence is by engaging in reciprocal, give-and-take exchanges. But this is a paradigm example of the kind of transactional thinking that undermines one's persuasiveness in the long run.

Focus solely on the "give." Simple as it may seem, habitually generous people are more persuasive. So get in the habit of giving things away in as many interactions as possible.

Some of the latest science backs me up. Human beings evolved to be generous, it turns out, because it was a reliable way to get people to cooperate. And in a real-world environment where people aren't always in a position to reciprocate, a default generosity is a proven way to earn people's trust and appreciation.

The more you look at your interactions with others as opportunities to give, the more you will recognize what's being asked of you or what you have to contribute. Giving breaks down into four categories:

1. Time and attention
2. Advice and recommendations
3. Compliments and recognition
4. Stuff

What's crucial is that no matter what you're giving away, it must be something you find valuable. Just as important, you can't expect anything in return. Being generous will make you a happier person and will create stronger relationships and bonds with those in your life. If you become the kind of person who exhibits a generous character, persuasiveness will be a natural by-product.

The returns that come from putting good things into the world will accrue with compound interest.

Chapter 5

# the pull of positivity

---

*The mind is everything. What you think you become.*

—Buddha

Broadly speaking, instances of persuasion fall into two categories: negative or positive.

Anytime a person tries to win someone over by evoking fear, hatred, disgust, or anxiety, they are engaging in negative persuasion. And, sadly, you don't need to look far in our culture to see these sorts of tactics in action. The paradigm case is the political attack ad that portrays one candidate as dangerous or evil. The goal of these ads is to make you so afraid or angry about the possibility of Candidate X winning that you can't help but vote for Candidate Y.

Just think of President Lyndon B. Johnson's famous "Daisy"

ad during the 1964 campaign, in which a three-year-old girl stands in a sunny field, birds chirping, as she plucks daisy petals one by one until, on the count of ten, a nuclear bomb detonates. "These are the stakes," we hear Johnson's voice say.[1] This ad aired only once, and was likely pivotal to Johnson's decisive defeat of Barry Goldwater. Although Goldwater's name is not mentioned once, the viewer thinks, "I better vote for this guy or I might die in a nasty nuclear war." This is successful fear-based persuasion.

Over fifty years later, Donald Trump went well beyond imaginative attack ads, resorting to straight-up playground-bully tactics by coining condescending names for each opponent who stood in his way: "Low Energy" Jeb Bush, "Weak" Ben Carson, "Crooked" Hillary Clinton, "Lyin'" Ted Cruz, "Little" Marco Rubio, "Pocahontas" for Elizabeth Warren, "Crazy" Joe Biden, and on and on.

Simple and consistent negative messages do work. In fact, they can be an incredibly powerful way to change people's minds or get them to the polls. But the question you have to ask is: Does the world need any more fear, hatred, anxiety, or anger in it? Of course not, we already have that in spades.

In fact, we are overdosing on anxiety. It's gone so negative that many people can't wait for the opportunity to step on someone else's head to move up. But most of us are good at heart, and if you are going to inspire any kind of emotion in another person, always go positive. Keep it healthy. Short gains can surely be made by cutting others down or smearing the competition, but this never works out in the long run.

Positive persuasion relies on life-affirming emotions to pull people to your position. Instead of reminding your audience of the dangers of a given choice, it fills them with a sense of excitement and opportunity. Make people feel good about their choices instead of bad about picking the wrong side.

Soulful persuasion is all about cultivating character—the kind of character that gives off positivity by default. Not the obnoxiously perky person who can't stop smiling, uses the phrase "no worries," and describes everything under the sun as "exciting." That's not positivity. That's phony bullshit. Nor am I talking about the person who indulges in wishful thinking and sees a silver lining in every cloud, even when there isn't one. I don't think that delusional positivity helps anybody. Obviously, it takes a hell of a lot more than happy thoughts to achieve your goals.

The kind of dispositionally positive person I am talking about is someone who gives their genuine positive emotions priority in everything they do and, as a consequence, leaves the people around them feeling just a little better. These positive emotions can run the gamut from joy and satisfaction to confidence, optimism, and gratitude.

None of which is to suggest that habitually positive people never feel bad. They can be moody or angry, like everybody else. Yet they train themselves to let their positive feelings guide their decisions, actions, comments, and thoughts the majority of the time. In this way, they display a kind of generosity—*a generosity of spirit.*

Will a predominantly positive disposition make you happier, healthier, more creative, or better in bed? Probably. But what we know for sure is that habitually positive individuals are the kind of people that others like having around. We seek them out when we need advice, have a problem, or need a job done. And we want them there with us when things are going well. We just like them. When they are there, they make things better.

But for our purposes, these are also the kinds of people we enjoy agreeing with.

## The Upshot of Positivity

We should prefer to spread uplifting, life-affirming emotions rather than the alternative. But how do you put that preference into action—especially if it is not in your nature? In many instances, it boils down to a simple and easy-to-follow rule: When in doubt, highlight the potential upside of a given decision, instead of fixating on the downside.

The basis of this rule isn't tough to understand. After all, which would you rather be told: that a certain workout regimen will make you less flabby and out-of-shape, or that it will help you feel healthier, have more energy, and look better on the beach? The first message reminds someone that they are overweight, while the second paints a picture of a brighter, more productive potential self.

Similarly, would you rather be told "You don't call your mother enough, so pick up the damn phone once in a while!" or "Your mom loves it when you call—it would mean so much to her if you gave her a ring and brightened her day"? The first message is a vehicle for guilt. The second is an invitation to do something good for someone you love.

Both might be effective at getting a desired result. But people who inspire guilt, anger, and fear aren't very pleasant to be around, and as we age, we avoid these types of people (unless, of course, they're related to us and we just have to suck it up and deal with it). And when you are playing the long game, you definitely don't want to be someone people feel compelled to avoid. Why make someone feel bad if you can help it?

Here are some examples of how you can turn a negative persuasive message into a positive one:

| NEGATIVE | POSITIVE |
| --- | --- |
| This product will make you less tired. | This product will give you more energy. |
| Smoking takes years off your life. | If you quit now, you'll live much longer. |
| Don't be stupid. | I know you're smarter than that. |
| If you don't donate, people will die. | Your donation can save lives. |
| This job will keep you out of bankruptcy. | This job will make you financially secure. |
| Failing to recycle destroys the planet. | Recycling has huge benefits for Mother Earth. |

From the standpoint of persuasion, positive messages are more effective at engaging audiences. That was the upshot of a 2008 study that looked at several decades of academic research on a single question: Are loss-framed persuasive messages ("You'll get skin cancer if you don't use sunscreen") more engaging than gain-framed messages ("Sunscreen makes your skin look healthier")? Plenty of work had been done over the years examining the engagement effects of different persuasive messages, yet nobody had bothered to consider all of those studies at once. That is, until Daniel O'Keefe and his colleague took up the task in 2008.[2]

Going into the study, the authors assumed that negative persuasive messages would be more engaging than positive ones. That assumption seemed safe at the time. There's simply no denying that the prospect of losing something important to us arouses powerful emotions like fear and anxiety. Such emotions have a way of focusing the mind and motivating action. So, one would expect negative messages to win handily in the competition for listener engagement. This is why campaign flacks continue to rely on political attack ads. And it's pretty much the basis for the entire insurance industry.

But O'Keefe and his colleague found something that they weren't expecting. After crunching the numbers from forty-two separate analyses published over the course of more than thirty years, the researchers discovered that positive, gain-based persuasive messages lead to "significantly greater message engagement" than negative ones.

When it comes time to sway people, positivity is your best friend.

## Positivity Is Contagious

One reason positivity has persuasive benefits is that it's highly contagious. In fact, it's pretty amazing how powerfully you can influence another person's outlook just by changing your own. This was made clear in another famous study from 1962 by psychologists Stanley Schachter and Jerome E. Singer.[3]

In their experiment, participants were injected with adrenaline, a chemical that causes increased heart rate, blood pressure, and breathing rate. The participants didn't know what drug they were receiving—the experimenters told them it was a drug for testing their eyesight. They were then asked to wait in a room with another person who was secretly in on the experiment. The goal of the study was to see how the mood of the people around us affects our perception of our own emotions.

In some cases, the person who was in on the experiment pretended to experience euphoria. Sure enough, this made the participants—who were amped up on adrenaline and didn't know it—more likely to report feeling euphoric. In another instance, the person on the inside acted angrily. When that happened, the participants who had received adrenaline were more likely to report feeling angry.

The study found that our own perceptions about how we feel have a lot to do with how others around us seem to feel. And if persuasion is the art of changing people's emotions and outlook, the ability to infect others with your own positivity is a very powerful tool.

Here is a recent practical example. I was stuck on the subway with my two sons on our way to a Yankees game. It quickly became clear that we were going to miss a big chunk of the game, as this train was not moving anywhere. As more and more time passed, my kids' sense of disappointment became palpable. It started with "No opening pitch!" and progressed to "We are going to miss two whole innings, Dad. This sucks!"

Now, part of me felt the same way. I had been looking forward to the game and wasn't thrilled that we were missing so much action. Had I indulged my feeling of disappointment, my kids would have sensed it, and a less-than-ideal situation would have gotten a lot worse as I joined in on the complaining. This is something we all naturally tend to do.

But in this instance, I chose to look at things in a more positive light. I was, after all, truly happy to be spending a fun night with my boys. I chose to treat our predicament as a kind of adventure. I started a game in which we made up stories about different people we saw on the subway car we were stuck on: "What do you think that guy does for a living? What is the name of his cat? Where did he grow up? At what age did she leave home, or did she ever leave? Would he join the circus?" We would take turns creating a fictional name and story for the stranger. We even made up a name for the game: Stranger Fiction. We were having so much fun being creative that by the time the train got moving, they barely noticed we had missed about an hour of the game. I had infected them with my own feelings of positivity.

I'm not always the hero of the story in cases like this—maybe only half the time. After a long day or a missed opportunity or a lost pitch, I can spiral out of control and become an asshole. But we all have the choice to use the pull of positivity to keep our negative emotions in check and sometimes, when we shine, even to elevate the experience.

## The Beer Test

As a rule, when it comes time to choose sides in a dispute or decide which person to trust, you're going to lean toward the person who engenders positive feelings in you. A lot of times, contemporary campaign politics is based on this basic insight.

When you cast a ballot or endorse a certain politician's views, you sometimes do it because of the way that person makes you feel—not because you've dug into the research and found that individual's positions more cogent than his or her opponent's. By the same token, even when you think your favorite politician is wrong about something, it can be painful to admit it. You'd rather agree with him or her than not. Donald Trump was able to convince a lot of Republican voters to change their views on big-ticket issues like trade tariffs and Russia—not on the merits, but because for some reason they were drawn to his reckless and braggadocious style and bullying tactics. You can also see these tactics quickly wear out their welcome. They don't last long.

However, it's no coincidence that in *most* recent presidential elections, the candidate considered more likable came out on top. This dynamic is called "the beer test," since the candidates are often competing to be the person voters would most like to have a beer with. In 2000, for example, opinion polls showed that George W. Bush was pretty evenly matched with Al Gore on the issues but had a significant lead on measures of likability. The same was true when he went up against John Kerry in 2004. Voters also liked Barack Obama a lot more than Mitt Romney in the run-up to the 2012 election.[4]

I must admit that the beer test works on me. At my company, I make a point of interviewing every single new hire, whether it's an office manager, a junior producer, or a creative director. This can be highly time-consuming. But it's worth it. By that point in the hiring process, many others have already determined that the person I'm interviewing is qualified for the gig. What I need to find out during our sit-down is whether they are someone that we will enjoy having around. Will they contribute to the culture? Will they be uniquely themselves, express their opinions, and give off the pull of positivity? In other words, would we like to have a beer with them at the end of a long day?

To figure this out, I'll ask them questions that invite them to let down their guard. I'll ask what adjectives friends would use to describe them, what they think their "advertising superpower" is, what kind of music they like, why they want to change jobs, what makes them excited to wake up and go to work, what they would do for fun if they didn't have to work, what three people they would want to have dinner with, and so on. My goal is to get them to cut loose a little so I can get a peek at their real personality. If they're the kind of person who shit-talks their previous employer or otherwise gives off a default negativity, I'm almost certainly going to pass, no matter how accomplished or talented they are.

The kinds of people you'd like around when you're in the hard times are always those who give off positivity, remind you how good things are, or are hopeful about how good things could be again. They lift your spirits.

## How Joe Biden Won Me Over

This insight was driven home to me a few years back when my agency was asked to take on an especially daunting challenge for one of the biggest clients in the known universe: the White House.

On the morning of April 29, 2014, I found myself in the Roosevelt Room sitting across from none other than Vice President Joe Biden. Over the course of more than an hour, he made a powerful case for why my agency and other partners in the room should join forces with the Obama administration to fundamentally reshape the way the public thinks about sexual assault on college campuses.

As Biden informed me, as well as representatives from a number of media and sports organizations—including *GQ*, Major League Baseball, and Funny or Die—roughly one in five women and one in sixteen men are sexually assaulted during their time at college. Those statistics still blow my mind every time I think about them. The Obama administration's Task Force to Protect Students from Sexual Assault, formed earlier that year, had announced some of its policy recommendations that morning, including the creation of federal training programs to teach school officials how to properly treat victims of sexual trauma. But, as Biden explained, the problem couldn't be solved through good policy alone.

Preventing campus rape, he said, would require a large-scale shift in how college students—and young men in particular—understood the issue. What the administration needed was a change in the culture. And Vice President Biden and his team had chosen my agency, Mekanism, to bring about that change through a national campaign that would need to launch in four months from that meeting.

On the merits, you might think this was a no-brainer. Of course Mekanism should sign on. But there were a number of considerations that gave me pause. First, we would need to work entirely for free. I also had absolutely no idea how our agency was going to pull this off—or how I was going to justify this mountain of unbillable work to our CFO. The vice president was asking for a massive national campaign on a highly sensitive cultural issue, executed with no budget, and ready to roll out in a few months.

Until then, Mekanism had been in the business of moving product, racking up clicks, and getting people to share our content—not effecting large-scale social change. In fact, the administration initially contacted us after Rachel Gerrol and Dave Moss from the PVBLIC Foundation, Biden advisor Greg Schultz, and Kyle Lierman from the White House Office of Public Engagement spotted an interesting piece of work on our agency's website. The client was Axe Body Spray, and the campaign, called "The Fixers," helped launch a new line of body wash aimed at college-age men. To reach that audience, Mekanism created a series of digital pranks and crude jokes you could perform on your friends. The work was as juvenile as it gets and would never fly in today's environment, but it was effective, and the products practically flew off the shelf.

Of course, creating work designed to sell products to college men looking to wash with scents to attract the opposite sex is a lot different from convincing these young men to stand up and protect the opposite sex from assaults. We'd also never done any pro bono work before, and had no experience negotiating a political operation as massive and complex as the White House and all of its constituents. If we failed, we wouldn't just be letting down millions of past and future sexual assault victims—we'd be dealing a very public political defeat to the president and vice president of the United States. We'd also go down in history as the agency that botched a major national campaign for one of the most media-savvy administrations in modern history.

There were plenty of reasons to play it safe and simply say no. But that thought never really crossed my mind. Sure, there was the allure of the White House—a building that was designed to intimidate whoever walked through its (Secret Service–guarded) doors. The real reason I said yes on the spot, however, was Joe Biden himself.

From the second he walked into the room, he practically glowed with good energy and positivity. He was gracious, jovial, and curious. He walked around the entire table and shook everyone's hand, looked them in the eye, and thanked them for taking time out of their day to be there with him. He talked without any hint of artificiality.

And even though he was discussing a genuinely distressing issue, he framed his entire pitch around the extraordinary opportunity that lay before us. We had a chance to use our skills and resources to prevent suffering and trauma and to address one of the most serious social problems to emerge in recent years. How often does that happen? Compared to what he was describing, my concerns about money, time frames, and reputational risk seemed petty and inconsequential. This was about changing rape culture and creating a movement on college campuses all across the country.

Biden could have easily played the guilt card. He might have pointed out that I was a well-to-do advertising man who spends most of his time worrying about ice cream, airlines, and entertainment companies. "Why don't you do something valuable for a change?" he could have asked, or "Why don't you try using advertising for good? Your industry could use it." Instead, he appealed to our positive emotions by getting us excited about the project and all of the good that could come from it. It was soulful persuasion.

In the end, we came through. The result was It's On Us, a national organization that continues to promote bystander intervention, educate the public about sexual consent, and support survivors of rape to this day. It's On Us is about educating the public; it is not about asking people not to commit assault, but about making it an issue that we all need to help tackle

through policy change, bystander intervention, and open communication. Since President Obama launched the campaign in
September 2014, over half a million people and organizations
have taken the It's On Us pledge to do their part in preventing
sexual assault on campus. Hundreds of colleges have released
original online content and hosted events to raise awareness of
the campus rape crisis in all fifty states. Hundreds of individuals
and groups have created PSAs to spread the campaign's message.
Celebrities including Jon Hamm, Questlove, and Lady Gaga
have loaned their voice to the movement. And over five hundred
schools have formed student advisory committees to address this
issue in almost every state.

It's On Us has also helped inspire lawmakers and public officials to act. In the summer of 2017, Pennsylvania governor Tom
Wolf announced six reforms aimed specifically at advancing the
principles of It's On Us, including a policy requiring colleges to
adopt an anonymous online system for reporting sexual assault.

That campaign stands as my proudest professional accomplishment. I wish it was solely the gravity of the issue that made
me sign on. That was a huge part of it. But in all honesty, what
got me to yes was Biden's naturally positive character, his ability
to evoke positive emotions in me and everyone else, and the way
he made us feel like we had an opportunity to accomplish something truly worthwhile and great. That's how he got me and my
agency to donate years of work for a worthy cause whose import
outweighed whatever practical business concerns that initially
held me back.

It turns out Trump was only half right. Biden is crazy—he's
just crazy positive. And his generosity of spirit infected us. Biden
harnessed the pull of positivity to help us reach millions of college students, change lives, and fight rape culture.

## How to Harness the Pull of Positivity

How does one go about developing a positive character? There are several habits that I've found useful in maintaining a positive frame of mind and giving off positive emotions, even in the toughest of circumstances.

### Grateful Practice

In particularly stressful times, it can be difficult to look on the bright side. Negative thoughts can feel real and immediate, while happier ones lose their potency when frustration takes over. Sometimes the pressure can be too overwhelming to sustain hopefulness. Keeping a positive outlook in these moments requires practice. And the way many people practice is by keeping a gratitude journal.

As we tell our boys, you've got to be great—but you've also got to be grateful. Every Sunday night we write down in our book three things for which we are individually grateful. I know this is not an earth-shattering idea. And I'm not the kind of guy who loves shouting out my "intentions" in a yoga class. But this practice has made a world of difference for me and my family. It resets you and gets you prepped for the week ahead. Ask people who practice this exercise and they will all tell you how effective it is. The conventional wisdom is to make it part of your daily morning ritual. Yours might be every Monday and Friday on your lunch break. But for me, once a week with the family is the perfect routine.

The things you write down can be big-ticket items like your good health, or landing a job, or just the fact that you're alive and kicking. But they can also be little things, like something nice your coworker said to you in the coffee room. What's helpful about writing these reflections in a notebook is that you can consult previous entries and jog your memory on truly trying days. It helps you go back and tap into those feelings when you seem lost and hopeless.

This is an exercise that takes less than ten minutes, and yet the effects can be dramatic. Keeping thoughts of gratitude on the surface of your mental life can help you realize that whatever might be going wrong today, on balance you've got a ton to be positive about.

## Criticize Constructively

It's an unavoidable fact of life that sometimes we need to criticize others, particularly in our professional lives. But there's a difference between constructive criticism that is positive and disparaging criticism that is laced with hostility or dismissiveness. If a criticism is worth making, there's usually a way to frame it positively.

Instead of "You got this fact wrong in the report," you can say, "This report is almost there, but can you double-check this fact? It doesn't seem quite right to me." Instead of "Your idea doesn't make sense," you can ask, "I don't get it—can you help me to understand it better?" This last one is something I use all the time. It puts the emphasis on me, not on the idea, and it also forces the person to articulate the concept in its simplest form.

Most of all, make sure the aim of any criticism is to help the other person improve—and that the link between your comment and that person's goals is made explicit. For instance, if a person takes too long to complete assignments, don't tell him to pick up the pace. Explain that he'll be able to take on bigger, more challenging, and more satisfying projects if he can work faster. You need to lead by example, no matter your position. And nobody needs more toxicity in their life. Don't contribute to it.

Overtly hostile or negative criticisms can also end up back-firing on you thanks to a phenomenon psychologists call *spontaneous trait transference*. This is when a person who attributes certain characteristics to someone else is perceived as having those exact traits. When you call someone disloyal, for instance, it's possible for people to view *you* as disloyal. The same goes for dishonesty, laziness, lack of imagination—you name it. This can happen even if the people you're speaking to know you pretty well. A study published in the *Journal of Personality and Social Psychology* found that "even familiar communicators became associated with, and attributed, the traits implied by their remarks."[5] Someone who sticks to simple, positive, and constructive criticisms, on the other hand, can end up using spontaneous trait transference to their advantage, and coming off as more positive as a result.

## Bad Can Turn Great

Meetings can be a drag. Some are truly fun and stimulating, but others are so painful you're amazed they aren't banned by the Geneva Conventions. Such meetings used to be the bane of my existence. These days, however, I see them as an opportunity to inject a little positivity where it is sorely needed.

I do this by going in with an open mind and bringing energy to the table. But most of all, I do it by reminding myself that every meeting could potentially turn into something great. This is the truth. You might be meeting with a low-level accountant, the HR professional in charge of health insurance, or an unpaid intern and hear something new or interesting that eventually leads to an amazing breakthrough. Usually this doesn't happen, but that doesn't mean it can't. And recognizing that this possibility exists is a great way to bring some positivity, optimism, and energy to an otherwise mundane situation.

I first met my Mekanism business partners, Tommy Means, Pete Caban, and Ian Kovalik, because Tommy called me by accident. He was patched through to me via a production company that I started, called Plan C. Tommy was calling a local San Francisco agency, trying to drum up some work for himself. When I got the call by mistake, I could have easily told him he had the wrong number and transferred him back to the receptionist. Instead, I treated this chance encounter as a potential opportunity. Turns out it was.

That incorrectly placed phone call led to a lifelong partnership. Instead of me being annoyed and dismissing Tommy, we engaged each other in conversation. And we haven't stopped talking since. An open mind on both sides allowed this happenstance to occur.

This kind of serendipity doesn't strike very often. But because I know that any chance encounter can turn into something life-changing, I make sure I bring my full positive energy to even the most trivial interaction. As Frank Zappa famously said, "A mind is like a parachute, it doesn't work if it isn't open."

## You Might Be Wrong

Part of maintaining an open mind is recognizing that on any given issue there's a chance you might be wrong. If I'm going into a meeting at work or having a discussion with my wife about an issue, I usually have an opinion at the outset. But people who go into conversations with an ironclad agenda don't convey positivity, instead they come off as adversarial. Trust me, I used to do this a lot—coming in hot to a meeting and looking to pick a fight.

One way to avoid this attitude is to go into every interaction willing to change your mind if someone comes to you with a better idea. If you're a high-ranking manager at your job and an entry-level employee has a suggestion that conflicts with your views, give them every opportunity to turn you around. Similarly, if your boss wants to take a course of action that goes against your assessment, assume that he or she knows something you don't, and try to assess the situation from that person's point of view.

You won't always be convinced. But your willingness to give the other person a fair hearing will be evident—and appreciated. Just as important, this kind of disposition will make you naturally more persuasive.

## Get Excited

As Schachter and Singer's adrenaline study showed, there's a fine line between a negative emotion like anger and a positive emotion like euphoria. The same can be said about two other feelings, anxiety and excitement.

Major events, whether personal or professional, can bring about a lot of anxiety. Think about the day before a big business meeting or job interview, presenting something in front of your class, or that moment right before you step onstage to give a toast before hundreds of people. In situations like that, it's common for people to tell you to "calm down" or "relax." But that's terrible advice. You can't turn off anxiety by sheer force of will. A better approach is to reframe that feeling as excitement—a sensation that, when you think about it, isn't so far off from nervousness.

A 2013 study by Harvard Business School researcher Alison Wood Brooks found that this technique can be amazingly effective at calming pre-performance jitters.[6] In that experiment, Brooks asked participants to sing a song using the Nintendo Wii video game Karaoke Revolution: "Glee" (who knows, maybe it's a favorite among experimental psychologists). Karaoke contestants were required to belt out the Journey classic "Don't Stop Believin'," and they were told that they would be judged based on how accurately they sang the lyrics.

Before this happened, though, the participants were asked how they felt and were required to respond with a randomly assigned answer: either "I am anxious" or "I am excited." They were also told that whichever of these answers they were assigned, they should do their best to believe it was true. In other words, people who were assigned "I am anxious" tried to interpret their feelings as anxiety, whereas the others tried to feel that they were excited. After that, they let rip with "Just a small-town girl, living in a lonely world . . ."

Crazy as it sounds, the participants who told themselves "I am excited" were consistently better at sticking to the lyrics. These individuals were able to interpret their heightened emotional state as positive instead of negative simply by talking to themselves ahead of time—and they performed better as a result.

This sort of emotional reappraisal isn't always possible, of course. If you're nervously awaiting the results of a medical test or rushing to catch an international flight, what you're feeling is anxiety, not excitement, and telling yourself anything different isn't going to do much good.

When our team at Mekanism is preparing for a big pitch, I make sure to give off excitement at the prospect of landing an awesome account—not anxiety about whether the potential client will like us, what our competition has in store, or how hard the work will be. The same is true when we're working around the clock to meet a deadline for a big campaign. It's an exhausting, high-pressure time. But it's also exhilarating. So rather than focus on how tired and strung out we are, I always try to emphasize how much of a rush it all is, and that we are in it together.

I could attempt to motivate the team by reminding them how much is at stake (like LBJ with the "Daisy" ad) or how disastrous it would be if we fell short. But honestly, it isn't as effective. Instead of emphasizing how stressful the situation is, we frame these scenarios as exciting opportunities—just as Biden did back in the Roosevelt Room.

 ## RECAP

Maintaining a generally positive disposition carries a wide range of benefits that, taken together, can make you far more persuasive. People who are habitually positive—who reliably base their thoughts, beliefs, comments, and actions on their positive emotions—are the kind of individuals you want to have around. Their positivity can be infectious, rubbing off on you and making it easier for you to focus on the more uplifting aspects of your own life. They are more likable and more soulful, and as a result, we feel compelled to take their side whenever possible.

But it takes practice and discipline for it to become second nature.

The main tenets are:

1. Be grateful.
2. Criticize constructively.
3. Bad can turn great.
4. You might be wrong.
5. Get excited.

Internalizing these helps ensure that you bring a constructive, optimistic, engaging demeanor to all of your interactions.

Remember, people surround themselves with people who reflect who they want to be and how they want to feel. Positivity breeds influence.

Chapter 6

# just a little respect

---

*Knowledge will give you power, but character will give*
*you respect.*

—Bruce Lee

Respect is a basic precondition for persuasion. If your
goal is to be influential but you fail to respect your audience,
you've forfeited the game before it has even begun.

When we feel even the smallest bit slighted, insulted, or
talked down to, we tend to close ourselves off. We shift into "us
versus them" mode and start seeing the disrespectful person as
our opponent or even our enemy. Just think of how many wars
have been ignited because one side disrespected the other.

One extreme and obscure example is known as the Pastry
War. In the 1820s, following Mexico's independence from Spain,
some rioting and fighting erupted on the streets of Mexico City,

causing predictable damage. A French pastry chef named Remontel had his bakery ransacked and all his pastries stolen. The French king, Louis Philippe, found out and demanded compensation of 600,000 pesos (the equivalent of about $30,000 today), all for a store and some pastries worth about 1,000 pesos (about $50 dollars). The Mexican Congress said, in essence, "No way are we paying that much for some pastries." The French navy began a blockade of key seaports in the Gulf of Mexico. Mexico declared war, and France and Mexico fought for four straight months. The confrontation resulted in the deaths of many soldiers. Eventually Mexico paid the 600,000 pesos and Remontel got a brand-new bakery. But by demanding, rather than persuading and respecting, much more was lost than gained on both sides over some French pastries. So when someone has a score to settle against you, they aren't likely to be won over to your way of seeing things through demands.

On the other hand, when someone treats us as equals, takes us seriously, and shows respect for our time, our intelligence, our point of view, or our attention, we tend to open ourselves up—if for no other reason than to return their courtesy. We do our best to give them a fair hearing. And when we open up, we let down our guard. That's exactly the mindset you want to see in someone you're hoping to persuade.

People crave respect more than just about anything else—especially in the workplace. In a survey of twenty thousand employees around the world by *Harvard Business Review*, being treated with respect by their superiors had a larger effect on workers than any other factor examined in the poll. It was seen as more important than feedback, opportunities for advancement, recognition, or even money.[1]

Consider an episode that occurred back in 2009 at the Orient

Road Jail in Florida. An officer at the facility, Deputy Ken Moon, was sitting at his desk when one of the inmates attacked him violently, putting him in a potentially deadly choke hold. The reason the deputy is still here today is that four other inmates came to his defense. One inmate, Jerry Dieguez Jr., punched the attacker to the ground. Another prisoner, David Schofield, grabbed the deputy's radio and called for help. Two other inmates, Hoang Vu and Terrell Carswell, joined the confrontation, and eventually Deputy Moon got loose.[2]

It's highly unusual for prisoners to protect the guard. When asked why they put themselves at risk to save Moon's life, it came down to respect. As one of the inmates put it, "Moon, he goes out of his way . . . even though he's an officer, he acts like a father figure."[3] The deputy had treated the inmates with respect and as equals. And as a result, they instinctively took his side, even though it was his job to keep them locked up. They protected him when his life was threatened.

Our deep sensitivity to respect is in part what underlies the most universal principle of human cooperation: the Golden Rule. If you want to get along in any social environment, you need to treat others as you want to be treated—with respect. So essential is this idea that it can be found in almost every civilization and religious system through the ages.

The ancient Athenian orator Isocrates instructed, "Do not do to others that which angers you when they do it to you."[4] Or as Sextus the Pythagorean put it, "What you do not want to happen to you, do not do it yourself either."[5] Aristotle was once asked how we should act toward others. He responded, "Exactly as we would they should behave to us."[6] In Judaism, the Torah tells us to "love thy neighbor as thyself."[7] That thought is echoed almost verbatim by Jesus in the New Testament.

A Buddhist collection of texts known as the Udanavarga includes the maxim "Hurt not others with that which pains yourself."[8] And an ancient Hindu epic, the Mahabharata, instructs, "One should never do that to another which one regards as injurious to one's own self. This, in brief, is the rule of dharma."[9] In Islam, the Prophet Muhammad is believed to have said, "That which you want for yourself, seek for mankind."[10]

The Golden Rule is the fundamental building block of civilization.

Without respect, civilization as we know it—much less persuasion of any kind—would be impossible.

Yet remembering to give others your respect habitually is not something that comes naturally to us. But if you put in the time, it can become second nature—part of your emotional muscle memory.

Most of the time, when we disrespect people, we are unaware of it. Human beings, it turns out, are much more sensitive to disrespectful gestures when they're directed at us than when we're doing the disrespecting. As Georgetown University management professor Christine Porath, an expert on civility in the workplace, has written, "The vast majority of disrespect stems from a lack of self-awareness. Only a masochistic 4 percent claim they are uncivil because it is fun and they can get away with it. More often people just do not realize how they affect others."[11] Since we all want respect, simple awareness and focus can actually go a long way toward achieving it.

It's also true that our digital technologies keep creating new opportunities to snub, dis, ignore, mansplain, condescend to, or straight-up insult our fellow human beings with unprecedented speed and regularity. A single ill-considered comment, blog post, photo, or tweet can offend millions of people around the globe—and destroy hard-earned reputations—in a matter of days, hours, or sometimes even minutes. This makes a respectful character both harder to develop and more important than ever to maintain.

## Respecting Others: Being Reliable

One key to being a respectful person is reliability. A reliable person is someone who does what they say they will and doesn't make promises they can't keep. You can count on them—which is another way of saying you can trust them. And when it comes to soulful persuasion, trust is everything. The most compelling argument, sales pitch, or advertising campaign in the world means nothing if you don't trust that the words that you're hearing will translate into action.

Breaking even the most inconsequential promise is enough to undermine your reliability and, in the process, disrespect someone. To take one easy example, say something unexpected and urgent comes up during a phone conversation, and you tell the person on the phone, "Actually, I need to call you right back." We say this all of the time, and most people on the receiving end are fine with it. But if you don't, in fact, call that person back, it can count against you.

While you might not think twice about breaking that promise, odds are the person you hung up on will—people are highly sensitive to any sign of disrespect. And by making an empty promise, you're telling that person that you only care about them when it's convenient.

Keeping even the smallest of promises is a pretty easy way to demonstrate your character and earn trust. Here are some habits that can reveal your reliability without your having to think about it.

## Don't "Promise"

If you're someone who uses words like "promise," "guarantee," or "certain," don't. Absolute terms like these, when thrown around too freely, can get you into trouble by putting you in a position where you have no choice but to break your word. People will understand if you tell them straight out that you can't guarantee a certain result.

## Ask for Time Before Committing

If you're even a little bit hesitant about making an ironclad commitment, no matter how large or small, ask for a day—or a week, or even an afternoon—to think it over to make sure you can come through. This will prevent you from overcommitting yourself. Just as important, it will give you the space to consider whether it's worth it to make this request a high priority—or whether you were caught up in the moment and trying to make the other person happy.

## Underpromise and Overdeliver

If a situation comes up when I need to guarantee a particular result, I always play it safe: I underpromise, so if something unexpected comes up that takes me off track, I can still make good on my word.

## Be on Time, Even if It Kills You

Punctuality is perhaps the easiest way to show someone respect and demonstrate that you're reliable. Sometimes this will mean cutting a meeting short so you can get to your next appointment on time. This is fine—people are much more forgiving of someone who needs to leave early because of a prior commitment than someone who stumbles in fifteen minutes late.

One way to stay punctual is to try to get to every appointment a few minutes early. Think about it: "On time" is a minute or two before the scheduled time. If your goal is to be just slightly early, you'll rarely be late. To be honest, it is one of my ongoing daily struggles that I am still trying to master.

## Respecting Time: The Lost Art of Being Present

It's been said that "80 percent of success is showing up."[12] Bringing your full self to every interaction is one of the purest forms of respect, particularly in an era when demands on our attention are multiplying by the second.

I have undiagnosed ADD. My mind is in constant motion—I'm always thinking about the next project, goal, post, pitch, dinner, and so on. Yes, you can overcome this condition with better living through nutrition and maybe even prescription drugs, but you can also train yourself to think in a way that forces your mind to be present when you need to be.

This skill involves dealing with the single biggest modern-day enemy to being present: your phone (though it's true of every other modern-day distraction we humans are not wired to handle). Here's a situation we're all familiar with: You're having a conversation with a friend, colleague, or acquaintance when, at some point in the exchange, the other person reaches for their phone. Maybe they're looking at a message that just came in, or checking to see if they missed a call. Perhaps they just remembered they needed to reply to a work email. Doesn't matter what the reason is. What matters is that in that moment the other person has officially disengaged from you and your conversation. They are no longer present. It is a sign of disrespect.

This kind of behavior is so common that there's even a term for it: "phubbing," short for "phone snubbing." A study by researchers from Tilburg University in the Netherlands examined the effect of phubbing on 104 students.[13] Each participant was paired with someone they had never met. Before the experiment began, these two strangers spent ten minutes getting to know each other.

Then each pair was assigned randomly to one of three different groups. In one group, the two were asked to have a conversation without any phones present. This was the "no phubbing" control group. In the second group, one of the participants was instructed to phub the other during the course of their conversation any time their phone sent out a notification. The researchers called this "reactive" phubbing. In the third group, one of the two conversation partners was asked to look at his or her phone every time they saw a light in the back of the room go on. Their partner couldn't see the light and didn't even know about this feature of the experiment, what the researchers called "proactive" phubbing. The goal of the experiment was to study how three different scenarios—no phubbing, phubbing after a phone message appeared, and unsolicited phubbing—affected the other person's feelings toward their conversation partner.

People who checked their phones were viewed as less polite

and less attentive than people who didn't. And, as you might expect, proactive phubbing elicited more negative emotions than reactive phubbing.

This wasn't an isolated result. A previous study by psychologists at the University of Kent found that people reacted negatively after simply watching a computer simulation of one person phubbing another.[14] Yup, that's right—even cartoon phubbing rubs us the wrong way. And a survey by professors at the University of Southern California revealed that 75 percent of people believe that checking messages or emails during client business meetings is entirely unacceptable. In that same poll, 87 percent of people gave a strong thumbs-down to answering a call during a meeting.[15]

## How to Divide Your Attention in a Digital World

There are plenty of situations where you need to be present in your current interaction and yet still need to be reachable by phone. Maybe your kid is sick, in which case going into digital blackout for a two-hour meeting is simply irresponsible. Maybe you're the point person on a time-sensitive project at work that's in a critical phase. Or maybe your boss is going through a crisis and can't wait all afternoon to hear back from you.

The question then becomes: How do you give the people you're talking to the respect they deserve, while still being available to people who aren't in the room? There are a few techniques you can try.

## Apologize in Advance

You're in a meeting with a client, a colleague, or even your boss, and you know beforehand that you need to be on call for some truly legitimate reason. In these cases, assume the person you're with is a reasonable human being, and bring them in on the situation. I usually say something like, "I know this might seem rude, but my kid is sick and I'm waiting to hear from the doctor, so I might need to briefly step out for a call or answer a message." Or "My roommate is having a crisis, and I may need to step out for a minute to help her." Whatever the reason you need to be reached, state it.

Doing this not only enables you to put the matter on hold—without feeling guilty or anxious—but also helps ensure that whoever is with you won't feel disrespected when you do, in fact, pick up your phone.

"I apologize, but I need to check this message" is a way to preserve a sense of respect and show that—despite this interruption—the person in the room is still your first priority. This might seem like an insignificant detail, but it can go a long way. Think of your phone as a potential relationship destroyer. When you reach for it, make sure you provide ample warning.

## Be Short, Sweet, and Specific

If you do get an important message in the middle of a face-to-face meeting, it isn't just the person in the room you need to be worried about offending. I'll sometimes get an anxious email from a client that demands an immediate reply. If I'm having coffee with another client, a colleague, or a friend, I might not have time to tap out a lengthy response. Here I run the risk of offending the client on the other end of the email—a person who expects me to be available 24/7, particularly when the shit hits the fan.

Let's assume that the issue at hand isn't something that requires me to rush away from the in-person meeting (it rarely is). Usually what the client is looking for is some assurance that I understand what's up and that everything is under control. So my strategy is to reply as quickly as possible—and to be short, to the point, and specific about when I'll be in touch. For instance, I'll write "We've got this under control. I'm in a meeting right now, but will call you in a few hours with a plan."

Replying immediately—or close to it—is gold for most people. When someone sends you a message and your reply instantly appears in their inbox, your attentiveness and thus your respect for the other person become clear.

## Announce You'll be Unavailable

If I'm going into a meeting at a time when I know someone might need me, I reach out to them first to let them know the situation—a quick email or message saying, "Hey, I'll be in a meeting for the next hour, but I'll be available anytime after that if you need to chat." Unless you're a trauma surgeon, it's rare that something comes up that can't wait an hour.

## How Being Present—and Demetri Martin—Kept Mekanism Going

A commitment to being present played a huge role in one of Mekanism's earliest successes. In 2006, Microsoft was getting ready to roll out its new operating system, Windows Vista, with a buzzy digital advertising campaign. At the time, Microsoft's ad agency, McCann Erickson, wasn't a digital powerhouse. So that shop's chief creative officer, Rob Bagot, reached out to Mekanism for reinforcements.

In those days, we were still a small-time operation based in San Francisco and specializing mainly in production. So getting to work with Microsoft was a huge deal for us. It was also our best hope of staying in business because, as was often the case in those early years, we were running on fumes. We needed this account to keep the lights on.

Our original concept, created by my partners Ian Kovalik, Pete Caban, and Tommy Means, was to build a digital campaign around a secret Illuminati-like society called *While You Were Sleeping*, which was rumored to include luminaries like Richard Branson, Stanley Kubrick, John Cleese, and Damien Hirst. Building on this idea, we would create a central hub for an online scavenger hunt that solicited new members for the club. Then we would establish a community-based site where candidates were encouraged to post insights, ideas, and creative points of view. It would become an exclusive social network.

This idea was nixed, and we were sent back to the drawing board with just a few words of direction—the campaign needed to be based on the concept of *clarity*, because the new operating system promised to clean the clutter and allow the user to work more freely.

We landed on an image of a transparent sheet, the kind used with overhead projectors, that you could write on and make shadow puppets against. Then Tommy remembered that there was a comedian who based his act around that very device—Demetri Martin. Demetri was blowing up on social media, which made him an ideal spokesperson for a product that was trying to appeal to a younger, hipper audience. Tommy envisioned a web series written by and starring Demetri as a person who has become overwhelmed by modern existence and can no longer deal with the massive amount of information bombarding him.

It's no exaggeration to say that, at that moment, Mekanism's future depended on convincing Demetri to be part of our digital campaign for Microsoft. But we hadn't yet talked to him, and just then we got some really bad news. Apple had just offered Demetri a lot of money to star in a commercial for Mac alongside author and Daily Show contributor John Hodgman. Hodgman would be the personification of a PC—a stodgy, nerdy-looking character, representing a Windows-based machine. Martin was slated to embody the cool, youthful Mac, a stand-in for Apple computers.

We had to try to talk Demetri out of this idea, to tell him, "You don't want to stand in front of a camera and read a script some advertising agency wrote for you. Everybody is going to know you as being a computer for the rest of your life." But Demetri was halfway around the world in Australia performing at the Melbourne Comedy Festival.

Now, we could have called him up on the phone and given him the hard sell from the other side of the planet. But it immediately occurred to us that a phone call wasn't going to do the trick. Nobody is going to walk away from a locked-down Apple campaign based on a phone call. To close a deal like this, we needed to be there in person. So we used some of Mekanism's last remaining funds to book thousands of dollars' worth of plane tickets from San Francisco to Melbourne.

Sure enough, Demetri was impressed that we'd made the

trip. It was an undeniable show of commitment to him and his comedy. Ultimately he said yes. Not only did Mekanism land the gig—and keep our doors open—but we were also catapulted into the advertising big leagues. I attribute a lot of our success that day in Australia to the simple fact that we showed up. No matter how great our creative was or how much Microsoft loved our ideas, this victory simply would not have happened if we had underestimated the value of being present and showing respect.

## Respecting Your Mistakes: Taking Responsibility

Speaking of guarantees, here's one that you can take to the bank: from time to time, you're going to step in it. You're going to say the wrong thing, inadvertently offend someone, fail to show sensitivity, make a mistake, make an ill-advised joke, or screw up socially in some other way. It might be a private failure only visible to your inner circle. But it could also be a very public social media misstep that captures the attention of everyone you know—and plenty of people you don't.

We are alive at a moment when a single thoughtless remark can damage reputations beyond repair. And it can all happen very fast. Learning to handle these inevitable crises wisely is absolutely critical. In the moment immediately following a social media gaffe—or even a private comment that backfires—people will form judgments of you that can't be unformed.

Those with genuinely persuasive characters can walk away from these episodes with their influence intact—and perhaps even strengthened. The key to negotiating these highly sensitive situations involves demonstrating your respect for your audience by taking responsibility for your words or actions, even if it is painful to do so.

## An Ounce of Prevention

The reason a single misguided tweet or LinkedIn post can cause your world to crash down on your head is that it can be seen by an amazing number of people. This raises the chances that your innocent message can be taken the wrong way. On top of that, social media content often lasts forever. And you just don't know who will happen upon your message years down the road, how they might interpret it, or where you might be in your life when it all goes down.

Disney fired the director of the Guardians of the Galaxy franchise, James Gunn, for some pretty disgusting tweets he wrote between 2008 and 2011. From the looks of it, the tweets—which mentioned everything from pedophilia and rape to AIDS and the Holocaust—were deliberately intended to push the envelope by saying the most offensive things Gunn could come up with.[16] He probably got a few laughs out of these comments at the time, and he never thought for a second they could hurt his career. The tweets had been deleted, but that didn't matter. By now everyone knows that, once something is online, it might as well be carved in stone. It looks like Gunn is back to work, but it took apologies and time for him to gain his footing again.

I like to be edgy sometimes with my comments to friends and family—but today I try never to step over the line. If I still end up offending someone, then at least I'm dealing with a person who knows me for me and who I hope won't judge me by these one or two mistakes.

## How to Survive a Social Catastrophe

We are all human, which means we are all going to screw up. It's just how we are wired and we will all make mistakes.

Prevention is all well and good, but even the most careful person is going to say the wrong thing at some point and have to pay the consequences. What then?

There's a whole industry set up to deal with these sorts of situations, and they use technical terms like "crisis management" and "damage control." But this kind of response is just tactical. And if you've worked to develop a good character—one that includes all of the traits I've discussed so far, including genuineness, long-game thinking, generosity, and respect—you shouldn't have to think so strategically. You shouldn't be trying to say the thing that best positions you to weather the coming storm. Instead, you should be looking for ways to display the kind of person you actually are, and let people decide for themselves what to make of you.

As the old Watergate-era saying goes, "It's not the crime, it's the cover-up." When people step out of line in a way that has serious social consequences, what usually does them in isn't the act itself but the way they react to it. President Bill Clinton wasn't impeached by the House of Representatives for what he did with a White House intern. He was impeached because he lied under oath and obstructed justice to cover his ass.[17]

When someone commits a major social error—like posting a stupid comment online, making an insensitive joke, or just lashing out in anger and deliberately insulting someone—the lasting damage comes from the revised impression of the person, a sense that for the first time we were exposed to a side of that individual we didn't know existed. It reminds us—perhaps even subconsciously—that the image this person presents is at best only part of the story, and at worst a thin façade hiding a nasty, hateful, ignorant, or malicious character. We feel duped and disrespected.

If that person then shifts into damage-control mode by denying, sugarcoating, or trying some other maneuver, they're just confirming our worst fears. After Congressman Anthony Weiner accidentally posted a shot of his crotch on Twitter, he went on TV to give some vague explanation about how his account was hacked. If his supporters had any intention of sticking by him before that charade, he squandered that goodwill by trying to pull one over on them. He ended up showing us a lot more of himself than he had intended.[18]

The only way to handle a situation gracefully is to show people your best self, openly, with all its flaws and strengths, and without qualification. This kind of response doesn't just show respect for your audience, it shows a respect for yourself. To do that, there are a few principles that are worth keeping in mind.

## Be Honest with Yourself

Did you just curse someone out online? Did you just make an insensitive remark at your friend's expense? Did you bring up a topic that, honest to God, you didn't know was a sensitive issue for someone in the room? Whatever caused the firestorm that's engulfing you, your first step should be to figure out how you wound up where you are.

Maybe you were just pissed off and, in a moment of weakness, wanted to hurt someone. Or you might have really thought you were being funny at the time, but now realize not everyone liked that joke. It's possible you simply lacked a crucial piece of information and wouldn't have said what you said had you known the facts.

For many of us, our first instinct is to be defensive, look for convenient excuses, or just play the denial card, Anthony Weiner–style. This kind of response shows disrespect not just for your audience but also for yourself. If you're willing to lie to yourself simply to avoid dealing with the real consequences of your actions, you're actually letting yourself down. The only way to improve is to recognize your own weaknesses and resolve to address them. If you lack the self-respect to do that, you certainly won't be able to show respect for others. The Golden Rule—treating others the way you'd like to be treated—only works if you treat yourself with the same respect in the first place.

We all cling to denial sometimes when things get hairy. The best—and most influential—among us fight off that instinct.

## Communicate That Insight Plainly and Quickly

Once you've singled out the real reason you screwed up so royally, figure out the clearest, most direct, most succinct way of stating it. Using too many words or couching your explanation in euphemisms only makes you look like you're hiding something. It might be as simple as saying, "I was angry and said something stupid and hurtful in the heat of the moment. That was wrong."

## Apologize—and Mean It

Now that you've explained yourself, the next words out of your mouth (or coming from your social media account) should be an apology.

What's the best way to show remorse? How do you phrase your apology to achieve maximum effect? I'll leave that to strategists and manipulators. My only advice is to follow the Golden Rule and give people the apology that you would want if you were on the other end of that offense. In other words, show some respect.

 ## RECAP

People have a highly developed sensitivity for even minor slights and offenses. And once you trip their disrespect alarm, getting them back on your side isn't usually in the cards. That's why a respectful disposition is an essential ingredient for a persuasive character.

How to be respectful comes down to three elements:

1. **RESPECT OTHERS:** Be reliable by doing what you say you will, no matter how small the commitment.

2. **RESPECT TIME:** Remain present in conversation (and if you can't, tell the audience why).

3. **RESPECT MISTAKES:** Admit it when you do screw up or do the wrong thing, and use these moments to demonstrate your thorough respect, generosity, and honesty by handling the situation gracefully and taking responsibility. If you want to remain influential, you need to use these situations as opportunities to show people the real you.

If you don't display a respectful attitude habitually, it's going to be hard to be soulfully persuasive.

# PRINCIPLE 2: GENEROUS

Generous people are more persuasive—it's really that simple. Such individuals seek to improve every circumstance they encounter, and they do it without concern for what they will get in return. This makes them more trustworthy, more magnetic, and more enjoyable to work with. They are the kinds of people we like having around. So if you develop this kind of character, you've already knocked down many of the barriers that get in the way of persuasion.

There are any number of paths to a generous character, but the following habits are the ones that have served me particularly well.

### Give Something Away in Every Interaction

Whenever you cross paths with someone, your goal should be to leave them just a little better off than they were. So make sure you give them something—a recommendation, a piece of advice, a compliment, a gift, or just your time and attention. Whatever you give, make sure it's genuine. This habit won't come naturally at first. But over time you'll start to see interactions in terms of other people's needs, which will make it far easier to recognize the best way to contribute something.

### Practice Positivity

Negative emotions can be a powerfully persuasive force. But the world doesn't need any more anxiety, fear, hatred, and divisiveness. So if you're going to wield influence, better to do it through positivity. And that process begins by learning to give your genuinely positive emotions a starring role in the way you approach the world.

If you can do that, the influence you'll achieve will be the kind that pulls people to your way of seeing things by filling them with a sense of possibility. Your persuasive abilities will flow from your generosity of character.

In practice, this means cultivating your sense of gratitude for the good things in your life, criticizing only for constructive reasons, recognizing that even the dreariest and most tedious interactions have the potential to result in something great, keeping an open mind, and reframing anxious situations as sources of excitement.

## Take Others Seriously by Showing Respect

Failing to respect your audience—their intelligence, beliefs, and experience—is the quickest way to sabotage any attempt at persuasion.

Fortunately, it's not all that difficult to avoid common sources of disrespect. By learning to keep your promises, being as present as possible, and admitting your mistakes quickly and sincerely, you'll have developed character traits that signal respect implicitly.

Generous people are soulfully persuasive people.

PRINCIPLE 3

# EMPATHETIC

If you
can't make sense of
why someone disagrees with
you, your odds of changing their mind
aren't very good. The most well-worded
speech or artfully produced advertisement won't
count for much if it doesn't speak to the values, concerns, and beliefs that matter most to your audience.
Moreover, a surface-level, intellectual understanding of
someone else's perspective won't do the trick. You need to
"get" your audience on an intuitive, emotional level. You need
to see things through their eyes and recognize what, exactly,
draws them to their particular opinions and beliefs. And that
requires empathy.
Empathetic people are skilled at overcoming divisions and
bringing people onto the same team. They are able to neu-
tralize the "us vs. them" thinking that gets in the way of
persuasion. They see people as fundamentally similar
and equal. They are natural collaborators who habitually forge connections with those around them
and find ways to work with others toward
common goals. In other words, they
are natural persuaders.

Chapter 7

# it's not me, it's us

---

*You can only understand people if you feel them in yourself.*

—John Steinbeck

By its nature, persuasion requires engagement with people you disagree with. If you're going to get anywhere, you need to first understand where your audience is coming from. You need to truly comprehend why they hold the positions they do, and get a sense of which of their beliefs are ironclad and which are negotiable. You need to meet them where they stand—not lecture them from a distance. This is why empathy is an absolutely essential trait for anyone hoping to practice soulful persuasion.

Empathy is the capacity to recognize and make sense of another person's feelings—or, as we often put it today, it's the ability to "get" another person. And it's hard to deny that, when someone else gets us, it's a whole lot easier to agree with them. That is why we have to attempt to put ourselves in the other person's shoes to truly understand them.

Unfortunately, empathy is in pretty short supply these days. There are plenty of theories why this is the case—could be social media algorithms or cable news or the fame monster. We are getting remarkably good at surrounding ourselves with ideas and arguments that confirm our preexisting views, and shutting out those voices that conflict with ours. A lot of us can go weeks without engaging with a worldview that is fundamentally different from ours.

One result of this new reality is that we're less and less capable of exercising empathy. If someone disagrees with us on an issue, we see that person as not just wrong or misinformed but as somehow unworthy, or even malicious. I'm not talking about fascists or white supremacists; I'm talking about people who just happen to belong to a different political party or hold a different opinion on an issue.

Back in 1960, only 4 percent of Democrats and 5 percent of Republicans admitted that they would feel "displeased" if their child married someone from outside their political party.[1] In those days, just because someone wasn't a fellow Democrat or a Republican didn't mean they weren't a good person. By 2016, 60 percent of people who strongly identify as Democrats and 63 percent of committed Republicans opposed interparty marriage.[2] And that was even before the Trump experiment.

If there's one thing this shift in attitudes reveals, it's a growing lack of empathy. It's not that we don't understand why someone would hold a different position on healthcare policy or immigration or tax reform—it's that, too often, we don't really try to understand. We assume the worst about our political opponents instead of seeing them as fellow human beings who have reached different conclusions on these complicated issues.

At root, this is the same crude in-group/out-group thinking that motivates racism, sexism, xenophobia, and other poisonous forms of discrimination. The only hope we have of living together in a diverse company, community, country, and world is if we are able to persuade each other and find common ground And without exercising empathy, that won't happen.

## Influence Through Empathy: George Orwell and Nellie Bly

One of my favorite examples of how empathy can change the way people think, and help reframe even the most divisive issues, involves President Barack Obama's response to the killing of Trayvon Martin, an African American teenager. Martin was shot to death on the night of February 26, 2012, in Sanford, Florida, by George Zimmerman, a member of the neighborhood watch.[3] The event brought the conversation about race in the United States to a fever pitch. Protests erupted around the country, and television newscasts were full of impassioned opinions about the circumstances surrounding the shooting, the symbolism of the event, and who, exactly, was to blame.

As the first African American president, Obama had a very fine line to walk when commenting on Martin's death in the weeks following the shooting. At the time, the killing was being investigated by the Justice Department, and as the federal government's top official—not to mention the most powerful political figure on the planet—the president had to be careful not to influence that investigation by casting judgment on the incident before all the facts had been gathered. At the same time, he knew he had to address the topic—he knew he had to use his bully pulpit to help shape the debate and tamp down the controversy that was pulling the nation apart.

He waited twenty-six days before uttering a word about the killing. But finally he couldn't hold his tongue any longer. And at a press conference on an unrelated matter (he was announcing Jim Yong Kim as his nominee for President of the World Bank), Obama got the question from a reporter—"Can you comment on the Trayvon Martin case, sir?" His answer is a study in influence through empathy:

> *I can only imagine what these parents are going through. And when I think about this boy, I think about my own kids. And I think every parent in America should be able to understand why it is absolutely imperative that we investigate every aspect of this, and that everybody pulls together—federal, state and local—to figure out exactly how this tragedy happened.*[4]

Then, he uttered a sentence that has gone down as one of the most famous of his presidency:

*"If I had a son, he'd look like Trayvon."*[5]

He took an event that, at that point, had become a wedge issue used to divide the country against itself, and he brought it back to something universal that everybody could relate to. Somebody's son had been killed. And by inviting the country to empathize with Trayvon's parents, he put us all on the same side for a brief moment. He reframed this story—which had become an abstraction, an allegory, a piece of political ammunition—as a tragedy that could happen to any one of us.

Now, of course Obama wasn't able to mend the social rifts created by racism, police brutality, gun violence, and all of the other polarizing issues surrounding this incident, and which since then have only gotten worse. But he sure as hell changed the way most of us understood the matter. And he did it by asking all of us to step into the shoes of Martin's parents and see all the parties involved as fellow human beings.

Obama was following a long tradition of political influencers who have exercised empathy as a tool for broadening people's perspective and helping them to see things differently. George Orwell used this technique in his first book, *Down and Out in Paris and London.* That 1933 memoir recounted the time Orwell spent living and working among the poorest in both cities. The result was a piece of writing that made it impossible to ignore the real human suffering—and profound dignity—of the least advantaged people in these places. It still stands as a landmark accomplishment in understanding the issue of homelessness. It remains so relevant, in fact, that as recently as the summer of 2018, actors and writers staged live theatrical events celebrating the book in both Paris and London.

Decades before Orwell brought to life the dismal lot of Europe's urban poor, the investigative journalist Nellie Bly got herself admitted to a mental asylum in 1887 in order to give a firsthand account of the atrocious treatment of the mentally ill in the United States. The articles she wrote at the end of the nineteenth century eventually became *Ten Days in the Mad-House,* a book that helped usher in long-needed reforms to that institution.[6]

Today, the most committed journalists continue to uphold the tradition of exposing readers to the uglier truths that many prefer to avoid by appealing to their innate sense of empathy.

I heard Michael Lewis, the author of bestsellers *Liar's Poker*, *Moneyball*, and *The Fifth Risk*, say the following at an industry event called Marketing 50:

> *If I told you that half a million people are dying in the Syrian civil war, you might shrug. But if I tell you a story about a specific ten-year-old boy—the same age as your son—that died walking home from school and I walked you through his story, you would be compelled to do something to stop it.*

In each of these cases, empathy and specificity proved far more effective in influencing people's opinions and reframing the conversation than any argument ever could.

## Blinded by the Right (and the Left)

To see how a lack of empathy can stand in the way of persuasion, let's look at a recent study by Matthew Feinberg, a professor at the University of Toronto's Rotman School of Management, and Stanford University sociologist Robb Willer. Over the course of several experiments, the researchers asked participants to develop arguments intended to win over their political opponents. For instance, liberal participants had to argue in favor of same-sex marriage in a way that would speak to conservative values. And conservatives had to do the same with the issue of making English the national language. The results weren't encouraging.

In the case of same-sex marriage, only 9 percent of liberals came up with arguments that were framed in terms of conservative values. The task was far from impossible. As the study notes, liberals could have built their case on a bedrock conservative principle like loyalty, arguing that, as Americans, gay men and women "deserve to stand alongside us."[7]

Only 8 percent of conservatives, meanwhile, could make a case for English as the national language that relied on liberal values. Again, this wasn't such a tall order. One could argue that adopting a single, official language would help combat discrimination.[8] But that would have required truly understanding where your ideological opponent was coming from—seeing the world through that person's eyes.

In some cases, study participants actually mounted arguments that openly attacked the morality of the opposing side. This happened even though they were specifically asked to come up with arguments that their political opposites would find convincing. You don't need to be a master persuader to know that casting your audience as villains isn't going to win converts.[9] What these political partisans lacked was the ability to see hot-button topics through the eyes of those who disagreed with them. They lacked empathy. And as a result, they were hopeless persuaders.

This widespread lack of empathy may be dispiriting, but it's also very fixable. Even if it's true that cable news, political flacks, and social media are undermining our ability to take an opposing perspective, that's not something we have a lot of control over.

What we can control is our own character.

By cultivating the ability to empathize, we can keep alive the possibility of persuading others—and even being persuaded by others ourselves. The first step in that process is learning to be habitually curious about people.

## Be Naturally Curious About Others

There's a time-honored piece of wisdom that says if you want to get on someone's good side, ask them about themselves. Inquire about their kids, what they did over the weekend, if they have any vacations coming up—that kind of thing. If you work in an office environment, you probably engage in this sort of talk all the time, whether as an icebreaker at the beginning of a meeting or while walking to the elevator. Rarely do we believe that the person asking these questions really cares about the answers; it's fairly well understood that this whole routine is just a performance.

On the whole, people enjoy talking about themselves and making themselves known in one way or another. But for a conversation to serve this purpose, people need to share things that are actually meaningful for them—and they need to get the sense that someone is actually interested. This is why it pays to be genuinely curious about other people and to let that curiosity drive your conversations. If you can develop this habit you'll get a glimpse of them you might not have otherwise seen. When that happens, you'll have given yourself the materials to understand their perspective.

Curiosity can be learned—it's a skill like anything else. And the reason we so often fail to realize this fact is that we're working from a mistaken view of what it means to be curious. Curiosity doesn't just boil down to caring about something. It's actually about suppressing your sense that you know everything worth knowing.

It's the reason we enjoy news stories that confirm our existing opinions, or surround ourselves with people who are like us and our friends. We believe, often subconsciously, that we know how the world works. So there's no need to seek out new information, or confront facts or people that get in the way of our tidy picture. This feeling of omniscience is a choice, of course. Our ignorance is always there, whether we acknowledge it or not—just like our heartbeat.

Curiosity takes flight when we recognize that we don't know everything about a person, an event, or a political issue. And once we internalize this gap in our knowledge, it becomes like an itch that we need to scratch. It raises questions that we need answered. We become naturally curious.

In the case of people specifically, a lack of curiosity usually results from the assumption that we've already met every kind of human being there is in the world, and that once we fit a new person into one of those categories, there's nothing much left to know about them. Becoming curious about other people is about flipping this emphasis, and there are several techniques for doing so.

## Treat People's Idiosyncrasies as Questions

Our natural impulse is to treat people's weird interests and quirks as ways to fit them into a specific box—especially when we don't share those passions or behaviors ourselves. If the person at the desk next to you has Burning Man photos all around their desk, your first instinct might be to label her a drug-taking, free-spirited, modern-day hippie. Or if your sister's boyfriend has a Star Trek screensaver, you might think he's an awkward sci-fi geek.

Shortcuts save time. But nobody likes to be typecast.

Instead of treating these small glimpses into someone's personality as answers to the question "What kind of person is this?," see them simply as new questions. Maybe you've never wanted to go to Burning Man and don't understand the appeal. You could be wrapped up in a misconception. That's an opportunity to learn something new—not only about that person but about a whole subculture.

Or maybe the person is a vegan, and you're a die-hard lover of medium-rare porterhouses. Maybe his eating habits stem from ideas you've never considered. Maybe he's also a meat-lover, but a health crisis forced him to change his ways. Or maybe he was raised that way. Odds are that if you express genuine interest, the person will respond openly and end up sharing something about himself that deepens your understanding.

This is a technique I learned from listening to the journalist and master interviewer Cal Fussman. As he explains it, when you ask people about subjects that really make them happy, "many will be grateful that your question made them think about an area that they are passionate about—and they'll generally want to dive deeper into that subject. The sense of comfort that you're creating will lead to a sense of trust."[10] Cal's focus is on questions to get to the real answers. He has built an entire career on asking the right questions.

Over time, you'll become more and more aware of how unpredictable the people around you can be, if you look for it. And once that insight takes hold, curiosity about others will follow naturally.

## Less Small Talk

This technique is the natural follow-up to the first one. Small talk can really suck the life out of an encounter or conversation, particularly if you're just going through the motions to be polite.

You know the kind of small talk I'm referring to: "How about this weather?" "Can you believe the traffic?" These sorts of comments rarely lead to interesting exchanges. And they're almost always a drag to respond to. How many interesting things are there really to say about the weather?

Instead, aim for a genuinely engaging conversation. There will be cases where an obvious question doesn't readily present itself. In those situations, I'll look for remarks or questions that can spark a deeper conversation. For instance, I'll share something about myself and then ask a question that invites them to do the same. I might say, "I spent all last night reading a book about Italian boxers in the 1930s—it really helped me clear my head after a long day. Do you have outlets like that?"

What you're doing is setting up a conversation about things that really matter to the people involved. You're skipping over the pleasantries and small talk and taking the fastest route to meaningful dialogue. If you do this correctly, you'll end up developing not just your curiosity but also your empathy.

## Think Outside the Group

Another reliable way to cultivate your interest in other people is to break out of your group and spend some time with people that you wouldn't normally hang out with. Your immediate community is no doubt full of interesting and compelling people. But if you really want to feel a sense of curiosity about other human beings, it helps to find situations where the people around you are unfamiliar in some more fundamental way.

This might be as simple as going to a party that normally you'd skip because your friends bailed. It could also mean accepting your friend's invitation to attend Sunday services at his church, even though you're Muslim or you aren't religious at all. Or maybe, instead of spending your vacation baking on a beach and sipping a cocktail, you follow in the footsteps of George Orwell and Nellie Bly and visit an unfamiliar part of the country with a culture that's unlike any you've encountered.

What, with luck, will become blatantly apparent is that these cultures are far more complex and surprising than anything you could have imagined. You'll start to recognize how little you really knew about your friend's church, or the Midwest, or the south of Spain. We all use these experiences as opportunities to deepen our understanding of our fellow human beings. Try to understand what motivates them, what their passions, fears, philosophies, and sources of meaning may be.

In short, ask questions you actually want the answers to.

## Listen More, Judge Less

The biggest barrier to listening well is judgment. We all tend to overemphasize information that confirms our existing views. Psychologists call this *confirmation bias.* And it's a powerful force that even the most fair-minded people succumb to all the time.

To be a good listener, however, you need to leave your own preoccupations and pet theories at the door, especially when you're talking to someone who holds a different view. Try getting a Red Sox fan to admit that the New York Yankees might have a better bullpen this season, even if it's an undeniable reality. They'll likely throw all kinds of cherry-picked facts at you to show why they're right, and totally ignore any facts that cut against their argument.

One way to counteract this tendency in yourself is to treat

conversations as opportunities to be proven wrong. There are several techniques to keep in mind as you learn to get into this mindset.

## Assume Genius

This has become something of a motto at Mekanism. We are constantly reminding our team that they should operate under the assumption that our clients are smarter than us. We always say our clients are geniuses. We use it as a safeguard against lazy thinking. If you know from the outset that the people you're serving know their stuff, you're going to be far more aware of the weak points in your own ideas. That's because you'll always be asking, "What would a smart, hyper-informed person think about this?" Once you adopt that mindset, it's easier to be honest with yourself about which ideas are rock-solid and which ones will buckle under pressure.

But this way of thinking is also critical to being a good listener. If you're engaging in a conversation with someone who disagrees with you, the question you should start with is "Why would a smart, informed person hold this position? What am I missing about this idea that makes it so alluring to someone who is as intelligent (or maybe more intelligent) than I am?"

## Give the Other Person All the Time They Need

Good listeners let the other person do a lot of the talking—that much you've heard before. But this rule isn't just a matter of being polite. In an exchange with someone who sees things differently, you should aim to get the best version of that person's position. Remember, you're trying to answer the question

"Why would a smart person feel this way?" Figuring this out requires you to give your interlocutor the time and space to make their thinking known as clearly and fully as possible.

## Admit When You Don't Understand Something

You might need clarification on a certain comment, or you might not have followed the person's reasoning from premise A to conclusion B. Maybe they've referred to a book or person or event that you've never heard of. Use these times to encourage the other person to rephrase their argument, provide important background information, or otherwise fill in the picture they're painting. This will let your conversation partner know they are being heard.

## Ask How the Other Person Came to Hold Their Beliefs

The beliefs we adopt are rarely based only on facts, logic, and argument. There's almost always a deeper story. And to get to that story, it helps to inquire how the person you're engaging with acquired their beliefs in the first place. Maybe it was an idea they were raised on. Perhaps they had a charismatic college professor who made a huge impression on them. Maybe they came to their conclusion after having a revelatory life experience. Look for signs of these deeper influences to ask about.

For instance, you and your boyfriend might disagree on what to do this weekend. He's dead set on going to a concert, while you'd rather go see a movie that just opened. By practicing empathy and asking questions that reveal your partner's true reason for wanting to go to the concert, you'll be much better situated to either go along with your partner or change his mind. You might learn that the band playing was your partner's favorite band in high school or college and has enormous sentimental value to him. With that information in hand, you might decide the concert is the better choice. Or you could point out that by going to that fabulous indie movie together, the two of you can make new memories.

## Restate Their Views in the Best Possible Light

Once the other person has laid out their position, take a swing at restating their view in terms that seem most intuitive to you. These restatements should be conversational, not confrontational. They often start with phrases like "So, what you're saying is . . ." or "Let me see if I've got you right. . . ."

You need to try your best not to misrepresent their position, but rather to make sure you've heard them. This is what philosophers call the *principle of charity*.[11] The idea here is that, if you're going to challenge someone's position, you need to start with the best version of it.

## Look for Common Ground

As you're listening to someone else's view, it's essential to look for aspects of their position that you can get down with. For me, these areas of common ground are usually the big-ticket values that underlie their opinion. So try to figure out what those are. Maybe their view on immigration comes down to fairness. Maybe it's about loyalty or generosity or sympathy. We all cherish these values to varying degrees. So if you can make the conversation about such universal concepts, you're far more likely to understand where the other person is coming from.

In that University of Toronto study, the reason participants in those experiments failed to formulate persuasive arguments is that they didn't connect with the core values behind their opponents' positions. Liberals failed to see which shared ideals were most important to conservatives, and vice versa. That's a mistake one can easily avoid with a bit of effort.

At Mekanism, the pitch is to get the prospective client talking about what's important to them—their values, their goals, their way of seeing the world and their company's place in it. What we're looking for are ideas that resonate and that we can use to inspire our own ideas. Ideally, we find a quote straight from the client that really captures where they are coming from.

When it comes time to present our ideas later in the process, we'll say, "There was something you mentioned in an earlier meeting that rang so true and got us thinking and led to this next idea . . ." This is often the most powerful thing we say to a potential client during a pitch. And that's because by repeating back to them a belief that we happen to share, we're letting them know that we get them and that they inspired us. And in a way, this gives them permission to embrace our work—or at least evaluate it with an open mind.

You want to aim to have a better understanding of what is truly driving the other person, what basic tenets they are least willing to abandon, and which ones they might consider revising. This will leave you far better able to state your own views in a way that doesn't push the other person away, but rather pulls them in.

They will feel that you get them. And they'll be right.

**RECAP**

Empathy and persuasion go hand in hand. If you're attempting to move someone, you damn well better understand where they are coming from. The ability to take someone else's perspective is hard enough when that person is already on your side. It's even harder when the person you're engaging with sees the world in a way that is fundamentally different than you do.

It's become so easy to stay inside our own bubbles—whether they are ideological, philosophical, cultural, or socioeconomic—that we're tragically out of practice at seeing things from new perspectives. And, as a result, our ability to persuade people has taken a real hit.

This doesn't need to be the case. We can decide to be more empathetic. And we can do it by adopting two goals:

1. Becoming naturally curious
2. Listening more, judging less

Your reason for developing empathy shouldn't be just about winning arguments, elections, or worldview grudge matches. The real reason is that it is the only way people from diverse backgrounds and belief systems will be able to come together in the long run.

If you've made the effort to become more curious about other people, to ask engaging questions, to listen without prejudice, and to adopt another's point of view, you'll have become exactly the kind of person that we all want to agree with.

Chapter 8

# the collaboration imperative

---

*If you would persuade, think of interest, not of reason.*

—Benjamin Franklin

If the person you're looking to persuade is already on your side—even in a trivial way—your chances of winning them over jump dramatically. That's why people who are natural collaborators also tend to be effective persuaders.

When you join forces with another person on some project—whether personal, professional, or recreational—you are by definition on the same side. When someone is already part of our team, we are more willing to hear them out, to trust their judgment, to be interested in their well-being, and to take on their views as our own.

In several landmark experiments in the early 1970s, psychologist Henri Tajfel and his colleagues separated people into two groups based on arbitrary factors, including a coin toss. Even though these teams were determined randomly, the "us versus them" mentality still took hold. People in each group showed a clear favoritism for their fellow group members when, in the experiment, they were asked to distribute points worth money. This bias toward their own team members existed even though the individuals in the experiment had never met their fellow participants and had no reason to believe they would ever see them again.[1]

Subconsciously, we recognize our collaborators as fundamentally similar to us. Their projects become our projects. And when we agree with the people on our team or do them a favor, we are affirming our previous decision to cooperate with them in the first place.

The value of collaboration and involvement is woven into our national character. The founders of our country waged the American Revolution in large part because they were unwilling to be governed by institutions and laws that they had no part in creating. "No taxation without representation" was the marketing slogan of the day. And it amounted to the demand that citizens be involved in the decisions of their government.

The result was the democracy that still defines us today—a form of government that derives its legitimacy from the fact that it is, at base, a collaboration. We may not agree with every law that gets passed or approve of the result of every election (that much is for sure). But even when we don't, we accept their legitimacy because we are involved in the process—we are collaborators. We have a voice through our vote. Democracy isn't perfect, but it's the best way we've figured out to get a motley, diverse group of citizens to agree to a set of laws. So it's as close to a perfect union as it gets.

The tendency to seek out collaboration and work constructively with others is an essential element of being persuasive.

## Collaboration Leads to Self-Persuasion

Collaboration isn't a technique for convincing people of your position—it's a technique for inspiring them to convince themselves. It is a way to induce others to engage in what researchers call *self-persuasion.*

According to the psychologist Elliot Aronson, with self-persuasion, "no direct attempt is made to convince anyone of anything. Rather, individuals find themselves in a circumstance where it becomes efficacious to convince themselves that a particular thing is the case."[2] As Aronson notes, what makes self-persuasion particularly effective is that "people are convinced that the motivation for change comes from within."[3] This isn't as crazy as it sounds. In a whole host of situations, we often act first and change our beliefs and attitudes after the fact in order to conform to our actions.

This was what the social psychologist Morton Deutsch found in his work from the 1950s. Deutsch and his research partner Mary Collins set out to understand the social dynamics at work between people of different races in public housing projects. They looked at two different kinds of projects, both consisting equally of white and black residents. In one kind of project, the races were segregated, with black and white residents living in separate buildings. In the other, buildings were integrated, with members of both groups living side by side in the same buildings.

These different living arrangements provided a perfect opportunity for Deutsch and Collins to test how racial integration can affect the prejudices and stereotypes that were dominant in that era. Encouraging these two groups to mix and mingle could end up inflaming racial tensions, motivating white residents to double down on their ingrained hatreds. But it could also mend the rifts that were tearing apart American life during that period. So, which would it be?

What they found was pretty remarkable. Simply bringing people of different races together eventually changed how they felt about one another. But those changes of heart came only after changes in the way these two groups acted. As Deutsch later commented, "Findings suggested that behavior change preceded attitudinal change: The white women in the integrated projects often behaved in an unprejudiced manner."[4] The act of living next to people of color, treating them as neighbors, and collaborating with them as fellow members of the community led white people in these projects to convince themselves that their old prejudiced beliefs were flat-out wrong.

A similar story can be told about one of the biggest shifts in public opinion in living memory: America's attitudes toward gay marriage. As recently as 2004, only 31 percent of Americans believed that people of the same sex should be allowed to marry.[5] Today, nearly seven in ten favor it.[6] Thanks to a 2015 Supreme Court decision, gay marriage is now the law of the land.[7] The debate went from completely hopeless to essentially settled in a little more than a decade.

There is still plenty of work to be done in protecting LGBTQ rights. But there's also no denying that the nation's about-face on the issue of same-sex marriage is unprecedented in our history. What caused public opinion on gay marriage to swing so dramatically in such a short period of time? After all, it took decades for Americans to change their minds on interracial marriage.[8]

Some people chalk it up to a generational shift. According to this theory, as younger, more tolerant people became a larger political force, the electorate became more open to same-sex marriage. That's part of it, but that doesn't explain it entirely. After all, the justices on the Supreme Court are all of an advanced age. The fact is, a lot of people pulled a total 180 on this issue incredibly quickly. According to one recent poll, 20 percent of Americans say their views on homosexuality have changed in the last few years.[9]

Americans, in other words, were persuaded. And my guess was that it wasn't well-worded op-ed pieces or cogent panel discussions on C-SPAN that got them to reevaluate their views. Those sorts of things rarely raise one's heart rate or open up a new way of thinking. Nor was it pride parades or campaign ads, which are usually just exercises in preaching to the converted.

What moved so many Americans to embrace same-sex marriage was self-persuasion. They came to realize that gay men and women are not fundamentally different from the rest of our fellow citizens. In part, this was the result of changes in the way homosexuality was portrayed on television and in the movies. But far more important in my estimation was that more and more of us came to know members of the LGBTQ community on a deep and personal level. Whereas in the 1990s just over 20 percent of Americans said they had a close friend or family member who was gay, today it's over 70 percent.[10]

And what this shift helped to make clear is that gay men and women are already our friends, our neighbors, our colleagues, our teachers, our children. They are on the "us" side of the "us/them" divide. Like the white women in the mixed-race projects studied by Deutsch, today's Americans realized that they are already collaborating with the LGBTQ community as fellow members of our communities. Once that was obvious, an astounding number of people persuaded themselves that their previous beliefs about same-sex marriage were just plain wrong. That's how powerful a force collaboration can be.

Not only can collaboration break down barriers and help us see each other as equals, but it can compel us to change our minds about fundamental issues more effectively than just an argument, slogan, or marketing campaign.

## How Pepsi Invited the Audience onto the World's Biggest Stage

Harnessing the persuasive benefits of collaboration is something that has been central to Mekanism's approach to advertising since our inception. And the clearest example of this comes from one of the boldest campaigns. Our client was Pepsi, a brand that is about as big as they come in ad land. And the campaign was created specifically for one of the most valuable pieces of media real estate in American culture: the Super Bowl halftime show.

The opportunity came about after a meeting I had with Simon Lowden, PepsiCo's former CMO. I had recently made the move from our San Francisco headquarters to our New York office, and one of the first things I did was reach out to Lowden. By that time, Mekanism already had a working relationship with Pepsi, thanks to a campaign we had done for the company's Brisk iced tea brand with Eminem. We were climbing, but still far enough down on the ad agency totem pole that I had never met Lowden. So I decided to make our sit-down count.

Early in the meeting, I asked him to name the biggest project and problem that he had in the hopper. When he told me that Pepsi was sponsoring the Super Bowl halftime show and they still hadn't exactly cracked the idea, my response was unequivocal: "We want to crack it."

A Super Bowl spot is still something every young agency dreams about. It's one of the few chances a brand has for reaching more than 100 million viewers simultaneously.[11] For that reason, buying just thirty seconds of airtime costs an average of more than $5 million, or more than $168,000 a second.[12] That's almost three times what the typical American makes in a year.[13] And that's just the entry fee for a simple thirty-second spot. It doesn't include the small fortune it takes to produce a truly great ad to fill that space.

The Super Bowl is also one of the few events left in which the audience is actually interested in watching commercials and primarily on old-school broadcast television. For many, in fact, the ads are one of the main reasons for tuning in. But this can be both a blessing and a curse for agencies. The Super Bowl advertising arms race has been escalating for so many years that it's getting more and more difficult to do something truly original. But that's exactly why I asked for a shot at the project—I knew that Mekanism's creative teams would come up with something original.

Lowden was semi-interested in seeing what we had to offer. And a few weeks later, we made our pitch. That year, Beyoncé Knowles, who was at the peak of her popularity, was headlining the halftime show. Our idea was to make the audience part of her elaborate stage show.

As we saw it, the Super Bowl rarely involves the spectators in any meaningful way. It's a venue for the players on the field, the halftime act, and the advertisers who hawk products. The audience is treated as a passive witness to the action, playing no real part in any of it. But we would design a campaign that asked fans to photograph themselves in specific poses and post them online. The photos would then be digitally stitched together to create a composite moving character that would be used as part of an introduction video montage prior to Beyoncé appearing onstage.

The faces of the people who submitted photos would be included along with those of celebrities like Jeff Gordon and Drew Brees. In other words, the audience would both produce and star in the halftime show as an opening act for Beyoncé—a creative collaboration on an unprecedented scale. And, by turning the spectators into collaborators in a historic media event, we'd be bringing them onto Pepsi's team.

(When I look back on it today, I notice that the idea bore more than a small resemblance to a technique used by the Kiss Army. The fact that I played an essential role in the band's publicity effort only deepened my own commitment to the band. I became more than just a Kiss enthusiast—I became a member of a nation of people who had a unique, personal connection to the band.)

Pepsi loved the halftime introduction idea. But there was a problem. A much bigger shop (and one of my former agencies), TBWA Chiat/Day, was Pepsi's agency of record, and they would go along with the idea only if they could take it over and produce it. To say that Chiat, a great agency, was the more established company is an understatement. This was the agency behind Apple's 1984 ad—easily the most celebrated Super Bowl spot ever produced, and arguably the best television advertisement ever created.

I said no. If Pepsi wanted our idea, I explained to Lowden, Mekanism had to produce the work from soup to nuts. It was a gamble, but it worked. Pepsi asked Chiat for alternative campaign ideas, but in this case none bested our concept. And ultimately, after the standoff, we got the gig.

We had eight weeks to produce a one-of-a-kind event on the world's biggest stage. By January, we had more than 120,000 submissions for the campaign. Thanks to the addition of a handful of influencers and celebrities with heavy social media presences who helped move things along, Pepsi received upward of 5.5 billion overall media impressions from the integrated viral campaign.

But the campaign was about more than page views, likes, and tweets. It was a way of using the power of collaboration to bring people into the Pepsi community—and, in so doing, to persuade them. And the next time one of the thousands and thousands of people who submitted photos has to decide between Coke or Pepsi, there's a strong chance that they'll side with the brand that offered people a chance to have their image on national television next to one of the biggest pop stars in history.

I dubbed this *involvement marketing*. The aim is to get your audience to be part of the campaign and to create a viral loop where you are marketing to your audience and your audience is also marketing on behalf of you. That's the kind of loyalty that can only be achieved by treating people not as an audience but as real collaborators.

## How to Be Collaborative

If collaboration can lay the groundwork for successful persuasion, then anybody hoping to develop a persuasive character would do well to adopt the habits of one of the greatest collaborators.

## Ask for Small Favors: The Ben Franklin Effect

Asking someone to do you a favor is a remarkably effective way of getting them on your team. I know, it seems counterintuitive. After all, when someone does you a solid—driving you to the airport or saving you a seat at a meeting—most of us feel like we're in that person's debt. We owe them one, not the other way around. This is certainly true. But there's more going on in these situations than we usually acknowledge.

When someone has done you a favor, they've entered into a collaboration with you. For just a moment, they've played a part in advancing some project of yours. And in many situations, this brief instance of involvement actually leads them to like you more than they otherwise would have.

Once you look for it, you'll notice this principle playing out all over the place. You might be working on a laptop at a local coffee shop and ask the stranger next to you to watch your computer while you run to the bathroom. When you get back, I'd bet that person will be far more willing to shoot the shit with you than before they did you the favor. Same is true of a new neighbor who helps you up the stairs with your stroller at the end of a long day.

This surprising dynamic was illustrated by Benjamin Franklin. In his autobiography, Franklin tells the story of being chosen as the clerk to the Pennsylvania General Assembly while in his early thirties. He landed the gig without any problem. The next year, when he was up for the position again, an antagonistic state lawmaker made an impassioned speech in which he argued for replacing Franklin. Ultimately, Franklin kept his job, but he wasn't crazy about having this unnamed legislator as an enemy.

Franklin, of course, was from a working-class family and hadn't even finished high school. This new rival, on the other hand, was both wealthy and formally educated. And since it was a safe bet that the man would hold a lot of sway in the state government one day soon, Franklin was determined to get on his good side. He decided against "gaining his favor by paying any servile respect to him." Instead, he flipped it and asked him for a favor.

As Franklin tells it: "Having heard that he had in his library a certain very scarce and curious book, I wrote a note to him, expressing my desire of perusing this particular book, and requesting he would do me the favor of lending it to me for a few days." The legislator agreed, impressed by the specific request. And, after a week, Franklin returned the book, and passed on another note expressing his deepest thanks.

The next time the two saw each other, the legislator actually spoke to Franklin—something the man had never done before. From then on, Franklin's once-enemy was eager to do him any favor he asked for. The two eventually became close friends right up until the man's death.

Franklin attributes this strategy to an "old maxim" he once heard (although I'd bet this one came from Ben himself): "He that has once done you a kindness will be more ready to do you another than he whom you yourself have obliged."[14] Today, this principle is called the *Ben Franklin effect*. By asking to simply borrow a book from this guy, Franklin turned him into a collaborator. The legislator, who before was openly hostile to Franklin, found himself invested in Ben's well-being. They were on the same team.

In the nearly three centuries since this episode took place, a number of studies have shown that Franklin was actually onto something. A 2015 study published in the *Journal of Social Psychology* found that, when an experiment participant was asked for help by a stranger, the participant ended up liking the stranger more afterward—and also felt closer to the stranger. What's interesting is that this same effect didn't occur when the participant helped the stranger without being asked.[15]

You shouldn't be shy about asking for small favors. If your cell phone dies while you're at work, instead of asking your close colleague to borrow her charger, try asking the new guy you haven't gotten to know yet. Or better yet, like Franklin, you might ask a person you recently locked horns with over a contentious workplace decision.

I know it sounds strange to treat, say, even loaning someone a notebook during a meeting as a collaboration. But that's kinda what it is. And instead of treating these small moments as inconveniences, you can see them as opportunities to forge a connection with a new person and get them on your team.

## Ask for Advice

Similar benefits can be derived from asking for advice—which, when you think about it, is just a special case of asking for a favor. Again, this cuts against our intuition. We tend to feel as if asking for advice shows weakness or insecurity. But that's the wrong way of looking at it. When you request someone's advice, you're asking them to contribute to something that's important to you. You're involving them in your project and inviting them to consider your interests for just a brief moment. In sharing their thoughts, they become your collaborator.

For evidence of this tendency, a study was conducted by researchers at the University of California, San Diego. Participants in that study read a description of a fictional restaurant and were asked to weigh in on the eatery in different ways. Some were asked for their opinion, others for their expectations, and others for their advice. In the end, those who provided advice were the most likely to want to eat at the restaurant.[16]

As the authors explain, "Soliciting advice tends to have an intimacy effect whereby the individual feels closer to the organization, resulting in increases in subsequent propensity to transact and engage with the organization."[17] Asking about someone's expectations, on the other hand, had exactly the opposite effect.

A willingness to ask for advice when the situation calls for it is an effective way of getting people on your side. This is true whether you're engaging your spouse, a professor, an intern at the office, or your superior. When you find yourself struggling with a decision that could use an outsider's take, seeking advice can both make your choice easier and get you in the good graces of your counselor. It shows vulnerability and creates a bond.

## Give Honest Encouragement

A great collaborator is the kind of person people want to kick around a new idea or preview a work-in-progress with. When someone knocks on my door with a new approach or business strategy or just an early-stage idea, I want to make sure they leave the interaction feeling encouraged, even if I didn't love what they were batting around. Most important, I want to do this without being dishonest about whether their idea is a good one.

That process begins by being genuinely grateful that this person came to you in the first place. Being someone's sounding board is a privilege, especially in a creative industry. Advertising is a business of ideas. And when someone is willing to make themselves vulnerable by airing an idea they aren't sure about, I want to make sure that they know that I'm honored they came to me.

The kind of feedback you offer is just as critical, of course. Encouraging someone is easy when the concept he or she is bouncing off of you is something you truly love—that's the best-case scenario. In those situations you get to express your genuine enthusiasm. Just as important, however, is that you are specific about what you like about the idea, that you point to areas of possible improvement, and maybe even offer your ideas about how to move forward. The overall message you want to leave the person with is "You're onto something."

Things get trickier when the idea being floated is a total nonstarter, or just not there yet. In those cases, I usually start by asking why, exactly, the person thinks their idea works. If you think the idea is a dog from top to bottom, then pretending to be positive can just come off as patronizing. If it's just not good, be up front about it. Sometimes ideas are just bad. But usually there's something worth praising even in the worst ideas.

When someone tells you their idea, they're inviting you to be a collaborator—and that's an opportunity you should never waste if your goal is to be persuasive.

## Think Outside the Silo

Another idea that we stress at Mekanism is that great contributions can come from anywhere, regardless of one's job description, level of seniority, or background. Great collaborators are less interested in these distinctions than in doing good work and creating things of value.

Up until the 1960s, advertising agencies took pains to separate talent into separate departments. Writers wrote, artists were in charge of images, and so on. Each department had a narrowly defined role, like an industrial factory. Creative collaboration was not only discouraged, it was purposely segregated. At many agencies, wordsmiths and picture-makers actually worked on different floors and rarely saw each other. The idea that something magical could come from letting inspired people with different skills mingle and collaborate hadn't taken hold.

Then, in the late 1950s and early 1960s, one agency, Doyle Dane Bernbach, began pairing writers and artists in two-person teams. That seemingly minor change unlocked something special—subversive, intelligent advertising work that rewrote the rules of the industry. The most famous example of this was a series of advertisements DDB did for Volkswagen, including a famous full-page ad featuring a tiny image of the VW Beetle above two words: "Think Small."[18]

Mekanism takes this idea even further by using a process our creative leaders developed that is deliberately designed to break down barriers within the organization. A lot of our work usually starts with a discussion. In that way, our approach is more like that of a comedy show writers' room than an advertising agency—a group of a dozen or so people brainstorming in a room for several hours at a clip. The creative leaders at Mekanism find this gets to the best work.

The reason we do it this way is simple: One of the things we specialize in creating is digital content and branded entertainment—the kind of thing that lends itself to shared social experiences. As it turns out, the rowdy, collaborative environment of a writers' room—itself a social experience of sorts—is perfect for inspiring these kinds of ideas. There is very little ego involved in the process. In fact, after a particularly productive brainstorm, it doesn't matter who was responsible for what idea. The entire room is the author.

Anybody at the company is free to pitch ideas. Seriously: anybody. If an assistant, an accountant, a coder, or an intern has a holy-shit creative idea, their input isn't just welcome—it's expected. One of my favorite examples of this collaborative spirit in action involves Mekanism's logo. You'd think that because we're a creative advertising firm, our company's signature image—the thing that's plastered on every business card, webpage, email, and hoodie—would have been the result of some scientific process involving focus groups and typeface experts. In fact, it came from the pen of a guy who, at the time, was an unpaid intern. His name is Richard Krolewicz.

Back in his intern days, some thirteen years ago, Richard's desk was right next to the door. And since, at the time, Mekanism's office wasn't marked, Richard spent a lot of time answering the door for people who knocked by mistake, or chasing down a UPS driver who couldn't find our office. Eventually he got tired of the hassle and decided to do something about it. He drew a simple sign that read "Mekanism" in block letters, similar to the title on the cover of a superhero comic.

When it came time to settle on a logo for the company, Mekanism did in fact hire a branding firm, which spat out dozens of different options. But the team had come to love Richard's sign so much that they threw it into the mix as well. Of all of the possible logos that the contractors floated, nothing beat Richard's off-the-cuff door sign. Didn't matter that it came from an intern—or, for that matter, that it was pulled together in a slapdash manner purely out of necessity. It was the best, it was simple, it was honest, and so we used it. In the process, the agency showed an intern that he was an indispensable part of the team. It's no coincidence that, in an industry where creatives are constantly moving between agencies, Richard is still with Mekanism to this day.

Becoming a natural collaborator often requires seeing past the formal distinctions that can keep people from joining forces and doing great work.

##  RECAP

Human beings have a natural tendency to see the world in terms of "us versus them." This can be one of the biggest barriers to persuasion. But it can also be a major advantage to master persuaders. That's because, in a whole host of situations, we are often predisposed to like and agree with people we see as part of our group in some sense—as one of us.

By developing the skills of a good collaborator and habitually seeking out opportunities to involve others in your projects, you'll be better situated to hold sway when it's time.

There are four collaborative skills for you to consider that are particularly powerful:

1. Ask for small favors.

2. Ask for advice.

3. Give honest encouragement.

4. Think outside the silo.

Becoming a more skilled collaborator is something that is worth doing in its own right, of course. It can lead to more meaningful relationships and unlock creative potential that would otherwise be inaccessible. But it's also a powerful component of the kind of personal character that pulls people in and helps them see that you are fundamentally similar.

It doesn't matter if you're seeking to persuade your significant other, your boss, or your next-door neighbor—if the other person has already come to see you as a collaborator, you'll be far more influential by default. This is an imperative.

Chapter 9

# common ground

---

*Hip-hop gave a generation a common ground that didn't require either race to lose anything; everyone gained.*

—Jay-Z

We spend a lot of time focusing on our differences in this country. Our national conversation seems based on the assumption that we all belong to radically different groups, whether it's college-educated city dwellers, first-generation immigrants, or everyone's favorite topic of discussion, millennials.

I spend a lot of time looking at market data that divides people up into precisely these sorts of categories. Sometimes these groupings can be useful. But just as often, thinking in these terms distracts us from a very obvious truth—that human beings are amazingly similar, and that our differences are a lot smaller than we think they are.

Think of it this way: Each one of us shares 99.9 percent of our DNA with every other human being on the planet.[1] We are, from the standpoint of genetics, almost entirely identical. But we spend a whole lot of time and energy fixating on the 0.1 percent that makes us different.

In the course of human history, it's pretty exceptional that such a large group of people have agreed on so much for so long. Not to mention the fact that we all want a country that is a safe place to live, work, go to school, run a business, and raise a family.

Our common humanity is easy to lose sight of, mostly because we are really good at dividing the world. But when it comes to developing a persuasive character, it's crucial that you habitually focus on the things that unite each of us, instead of the things that divide us.

A disposition like this is essential to being approachable, relatable, and capable of talking to every person as an equal—regardless of each individual's background, social status, wealth, age, gender, or any other fact about them. When you naturally see people as members of your team, others sense it and are willing to do the same.

## The Benefits of Breaking Down Fences

I'm pretty comfortable talking to just about anybody. Unlike being punctual, this is an ability that came naturally to me from an early age.

One night when I was eight years old, as my father likes to recount, my parents were putting dinner on the table in my childhood home. My father called upstairs for me and my sister to come and eat—same as every night. My sister, Stacey, headed right down, as she always had. But I was MIA. Dad and Mom got annoyed. And after calling my name a few more times, my dad came up the stairs to tell me to get my ass down to dinner. It was then that he realized I wasn't in my room. I wasn't even in the house.

When he ran out to check the backyard, he heard my voice coming from the yard next to ours. He peeked over the fence and found me on the back porch next door, chatting with our neighbor Gil—who was in his mid-thirties—about football. Gil and I had been at it for a while. When I spotted my dad I nonchalantly said: "Hi, Dad. Were you looking for me? Sorry, I was just conversing with Gil about how much the Jets suck this year."

I don't remember the details, but I do remember my dad was a little flummoxed by an eight-year-old having an in-depth conversation with an adult. It didn't strike me as odd at the time. I didn't really notice the age difference. I didn't see him as an elder, and he didn't talk to me like a kid; we treated each other like equals. We were focusing on the things we had in common, and not those things that separated us—like the three decades he had on me. Not an earth-shattering story, but it exemplifies that when we put aside our differences and focus on our shared passions, amazing things can happen.

Just look at the development of hip-hop over the last forty years. The art form started in the South Bronx during the 1970s, when DJ Kool Herc would spin records at parties in the rec room of his apartment on Sedgwick Avenue.[2] That style was taken up by other local DJs, such as Jazzy Jay and Grandmaster Flash. And in just a few years, a combination of isolated percussion breaks, rapping, and other elements such as break-dancing had made hip-hop into a distinct form of African American culture in America.

It didn't take long for artists of other races to embrace hip-hop and make it their own. In the mid-1980s, a group of Jewish kids from New York—the Beastie Boys—combined hip-hop with elements of punk rock, with the help of producers Russell Simmons, a black entrepreneur from Queens, and Rick Rubin, a white guy from Long Island.[3] All suburban kids everywhere could recite every lyric: "Your mom busted in and said, 'What's that noise?' / Aw, Mom, you're just jealous it's the Beastie Boys." That same decade saw one of the most celebrated hip-hop groups in the history of the genre, Run-DMC, collaborate with classic blues hard rock band Aerosmith.[4]

Hip-hop didn't just transcend race in America—it quickly went global. Today, the art form is practiced everywhere from France and Russia to South Korea and Sri Lanka.[5] It is, as Jay-Z put it, "a common ground that didn't require either race to lose anything; everyone gained."[6] And it wouldn't have been possible if people from different backgrounds, races, and nationalities hadn't seen past their differences and found aspects of each other's culture that were shared and admired by all. What started in an apartment in the South Bronx has now become the most popular genre of music.

Not everybody engages easily with people they perceive as dramatically different from themselves. A lot of folks have trouble talking to higher-ups at their workplace, or people from different countries or cultures. Some strain to have deep conversations with anyone who isn't a close friend. If the person you are talking to can sense from the get-go that you are struggling to see them as equal, then you're not going to hold much sway with them.

Some practices will of course come naturally to you, while you have to work at others. I've always had a knack for being able to talk to anyone. But I had to work really hard at storytelling, and I continue to work at being present. These things do not come easily to me at all.

The path to becoming more approachable and better at conversing with a wider range of people starts with adopting an outlook that emphasizes human commonalities, and applying this outlook consistently. This means recognizing that we are all pretty much the same when it comes to the things that matter most.

## Social Identity

Being persuasive has a lot to do with whether the person you're addressing recognizes you as a member of their team in some sense. To put it in different terms, it depends on whether you and your audience share what psychologists call a "social identity"—the part of a person's self-image that is defined by which groups he or she belongs to.

There are a number of reasons this is true. As communication researchers Nick Joyce and Jake Harwood of the University of Arizona point out, "The people with whom we share significant social identities are more likely to share our perspective, and to know things that are useful to us." On top of that, they note that "if you and I constitute a 'we,' this implies a shared interest, which decreases the probability that you will give me unreliable or false information. For these reasons . . . shared social identity is directly associated with persuasion."[7]

Luckily, there are a nearly infinite number of ways that we can share a social identity, if we look for them. Depending on the context, a shared social identity can be based on anything from a shared language or a shared hobby to a shared age or a common city or state of origin. An outlook that emphasizes commonalities is more likely to bring these shared personal dimensions to the fore in our interactions with others.

This is exactly what happened in my exchange with my neighbor as a precocious eight-year-old. I engaged him as a sports fan, not as a runny-nosed kid, and—at least during that conversation—that was how he saw me. He didn't stop seeing me as a child, but that part of my identity faded into the background (until I got yelled at by my father for missing dinner).

One famous story that demonstrates this dynamic comes from World War I, in an episode known as Silent Night or the Christmas Truce. It's one of those events that, had you seen it in a movie or read it in a book, you would think it was a complete fantasy. But it happened. And the fact that it is real reveals something powerful about our shared humanity

In the winter of 1914, after four months of fighting in the trenches, French, Belgian, and English troops and their German foes on the Western Front stopped trying to kill each other for just a day and instead celebrated Christmas together. According to some stories, this remarkable event actually began on Christmas Eve, when one side heard the other singing Christmas carols. As one British soldier later recalled:

*The Germans would sing one of their carols and then we would sing one of ours, until when we started up "O Come, All Ye Faithful" the Germans immediately joined in singing the same*

*hymn to the Latin words Adeste Fideles. And I thought, well,
this is really a most extraordinary thing—two nations both singing the same carol in the middle of a war.*[8]

At some point the next morning, Christmas day, soldiers
from both sides worked up the courage to do the unthinkable:
crawl out from the trenches, greet members of the opposing
army, and wish them a merry Christmas. Pretty soon the men
were chatting, even exchanging gifts, burying each other's dead,
and, according to some accounts, kicking around a soccer ball
they made themselves.[9]

Remember, this was one of the most brutal wars in the history of humanity. And not long after the brief Christmas truce,
these men were once again doing their best to kill each other
in a war that ultimately took twenty million lives and wounded
another twenty-one million military personnel and civilians.[10]
But even in this extreme situation, something as simple as a
Christmas carol was enough to make these soldiers shift their
perspective for a time and see each other not as mortal enemies
but as fellow human beings who would rather be home celebrating the holidays than in the trenches fighting for their lives. If
this can happen in the heat of a world war, it can certainly happen in our own everyday interactions.

Of course, embracing a worldview that prioritizes our similarities isn't easy. One reason for that, as Peter Kaufman, a sociologist at the State University of New York, New Paltz, writes,
is that "we are socialized to focus much more on our differences
than our commonalities." But our differences, he points out, are
mostly socially constructed.[11]

Kaufman has been working to change this fact by inviting
students to participate in the *Similarities Project*. A few years back,

he brought a group of college students to meet up with a class of third graders. These are two groups that most wouldn't expect to have a lot in common. Just think of how much you changed between the ages of eight and twenty. For a lot of us, this is the decade where we change the most, as we transition from childhood into adulthood.

Yet when he put these two groups together and asked them to list the things they share in common, they were able to identify over forty similarities in less than an hour.[12] These similarities ranged from "We all have brains" and "We all like to play games" to "We all get sad" and "We all need love."

It's tempting to see these commonalities as superficial. But really, they are far more fundamental than the differences we usually focus on—like where we were born, what kind of music we like, or what sports franchise we root for. As Kaufman writes, "There is nothing inherent, natural, or essential about these differences. We humans have defined them, created them, emphasized them, and eventually, have fought or oppressed each other over them." Our similarities, on the other hand, are much more basic to who we are.[13]

And just as we have learned to define ourselves by our differences, we can learn to see each other for the things we share in common—if only we choose to do so.

## How Dollar Shave Club Used Common Threads to Slay a Corporate Giant

To see how focusing on commonalities can be a powerful tool of persuasion, let's look at one of my favorite marketing successes of recent years, the rise of e-commerce juggernaut Dollar

Shave Club. The company was started in 2012 by Michael Dubin as an online subscription service that delivers low-cost razor cartridges to customers every month. It has since grown into a wildly successful brand that was bought by Unilever for $1 billion.[14]

Dubin had zero experience in the razor business before launching the company. What started him down that path was a realization he had in the early 2000s. As a recent college graduate working as an NBC page, Dubin felt downright resentful every time he headed to the Rockefeller Center Duane Reade for a fresh clip of Gillette Mach 3s. "Even when I was out of razors," he remembers, "I wouldn't want to go and buy them at the store, because it was such a frustrating, awkward experience." Go into your local chain drugstore and it's easy to understand this sensation. For one, cartridges are outrageously expensive for what they are. A four-pack can cost more than $20.

There is really only one reason that these cartridges cost so much. Until recently, Gillette—which is owned by Proctor & Gamble—held a near-monopoly on the U.S. razor market. And like any good cartel, the company kept prices high because it could. If you didn't like it, you were welcome to grow a beard (which many in Brooklyn did).

Sure, P&G tried to justify their exorbitant prices by pointing to their R&D and proprietary technology. Their advertising seemed to suggest that Gillette's latest razor—with its vibrating handle and multiple blades—was the pinnacle of modern engineering. Most TV spots feature CGI animations that seem to reveal the science behind the latest overpriced throwaway blade—each of which promised to give a closer shave than the last. Usually a manly sounding narrator reads copy about how revolutionary the sixth blade is.

The Gillette ads featuring Roger Federer were especially mystifying. One spot shows the tennis star shaving, shirtless, before taking the court. The voice-over explains that "on match day, you don't leave anything to chance" before hawking a "limited-edition" Gillette Fusion ProGlide. You know, for razor collectors.

It wasn't until 2010 that Dubin began to see the high cost of these products as something other than an immutable fact of life. During a holiday party, he found himself making small talk with Mark Levine, the father of his friend's fiancée. Somehow the topic of shaving came up, and the two commiserated over just how expensive it was to buy a pack of razor cartridges. As luck would have it, Levine had acquired a warehouse full of surplus twin razors a few years earlier. His original plan had been to sell them to drugstores, but that hadn't panned out. Dubin immediately saw an opportunity to solve an everyday problem that most men take for granted.

Dubin set about creating a brand that focused on a common experience shared by all men. Instead of treating consumers as an afterthought, he would make them primary to the company's mission. Instead of depicting razors like high-tech wonders designed in top-secret laboratories, he would portray them as what everybody knew they were—basic necessities that shouldn't cost a fortune. He wouldn't lock them in a box in some sad, fluorescently lit drugstore; he'd deliver them to his customers' door every month by subscription, without them ever having to think about it. And instead of acting like a giant, faceless corporation, his company would use every opportunity to forge a personal relationship with customers.

To introduce his brand to the world, he posted a YouTube video that, to this day, stands as one of the greatest pieces of viral marketing ever made. The video begins with Dubin looking directly at the camera and introducing himself. "I'm Mike, founder of DollarShaveClub.com," he says. "What is DollarShaveClub.com? Well, for a dollar a month we send high-quality razors right to your door. Yeah! A dollar! Are the blades any good? No, our blades are f——g great."

Among other things, the ad is laugh-out-loud funny. And like a lot of great comedy, the video is built on a simple, everyday truth—in this case, the fact that razor cartridges cost way more than they should. As Dubin explained it to me, "What we did was give people a social asset to share with their friends about this very frustrating fact of life that they all talk about."

But most important, the spot breaks down the barrier between seller and buyer by treating customers as no different from Dubin himself. As he puts it in the video, "Do you like spending twenty dollars a month on brand-name razors? Nineteen go to Roger Federer." The implications were clear and powerful: Roger Federer is an unapproachable athletic demigod who has probably never been in a CVS in his life. Michael Dubin is no different from you or me. And he's willing to put his finger on everyday truths that all men have been living with for years.

This uncanny ability to speak directly to customers on a personal level has made Dollar Shave Club a serious threat to its corporate competitors. It's no coincidence that Proctor & Gamble launched its own subscription service, Gillette Shave Club—ripping off DSC's name—in an attempt to horn in on Dubin's success.

With Dollar Shave Club, Dubin has managed to give one of the biggest, most powerful corporations on the planet a run for its money in a market that, just a few years ago, P&G almost completely monopolized. And he did it by looking his customers in the eye and showing that he was just like them.

## Control the Necker Cube

Shifting from an outlook that emphasizes the differences between us to one that emphasizes our commonalities is a bit like the old two-dimensional Necker cube drawing everyone used to doodle in their school notebooks.

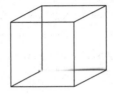

Look at it one way, and the square on the lower left is in the front of the cube. Look at it another way, however, and it's in the back of the cube. Both are valid ways of viewing the image. But it's impossible to see the picture both ways at the same time. More important, once you've recognized that there are two ways of viewing the image, you can switch back and forth between the two perspectives at will. Nothing about the picture changes—it was printed on the page long before you even bought this book. What changes is how you interpret what's in front of you.

The same goes for how you see other people. You can see them as a collection of attributes and identities that are different from yours—they have a different gender, speak a different language, have a different job, and so on. Or you can see them as a collection of features that they share in common with you—and, in some cases, as a collection of universal human characteristics ("We all need love"). Like the cube, once you recognize this fact, it becomes a lot easier to switch back and forth between the two perspectives.

It becomes an ability that you are in complete control of.

Now, in the case of the cube, the first time you see it, you're likely to naturally favor one of the two options (either the left square is in front or it's in back). It's only after thinking that you can switch to the other perspective. And the same is true of our view of others. For some, their first-blush view of others is the "difference" view—even though they can shift to the "similarity" view with a little bit of effort. Ideally, your goal should be to flip this tendency, so that your first, unconsidered impression of other people is one in which your commonalities are at the forefront, and your differences are only apparent if you really look for them.

For one, it's a great way to get over any anxiety you might have about striking up a conversation with someone you perceive as a superior. We all get nervous talking to a good-looking person we are attracted to or interviewing for a job we really want. This makes us self-conscious, and maybe a little tongue-tied. Needless to say, when you stumble over your own words, it's hard to be persuasive. Someone who is skilled at seeing others as no different from themselves is far less likely to get the sweats.

Similarly, a habitual emphasis on commonalities can help quell any anxieties your conversation partner might have going into the talk. In my case, when someone is nervous about walking into my office, their anxiety doesn't last very long since they can sense early on that I see them as an equal and that talking to me is not much different from talking with the coworker who sits next to them.

A disposition that puts people at ease and makes it easy for them to open up will always improve your chances of finding the common ground. This commonality-based outlook also helps guide conversations toward topics, values, experiences, and other personal details that you have in common with the other person, often without your trying. When this happens, it becomes obvious to whomever you're talking with that the two of you are on the same side.

## How to Find the Common Ground

### Make the Choice

The first step toward adopting a commonality-based outlook is to make the choice to see people as mostly similar to you. Remember, you can switch back and forth between different versions of the Necker cube at will, but only if you decide to do so. And the same is true about the way we view other people. If you are prone to seeing differences, make the decision to fight this tendency.

You might be having a disagreement with another parent at your kid's school, and think, "That guy doesn't know what he's talking about." Or perhaps a coworker of yours has a different opinion about a project you're working on, and your response is, "That woman has got it all wrong." We instinctively see the person on the other side of the dispute as separate from us. We interpret them as "that" man or "those" people. And we do it without thinking.

Ridding your thinking of this kind of framing is a bit like unlearning a grammatical error that you habitually make. Develop a keen eye for when you're adopting this kind of difference-based outlook, and shift the Necker cube.

## Practice Seeing Shared Traits

If you want to get better at seeing similarities instead of differences, you need to practice. One simple way to do this is to steal a page from the *Similarities Project* and do what Peter Kaufman had those college students and third graders do.

Start by thinking of a person in your life whom you see as radically different from yourself. Could be a cousin, someone at school, your sister-in-law, your dentist—anybody. It just needs to be a person you think of as obviously unlike you. Then make a mental list of all the things you have in common. If you look closely, you will often be surprised at just how many things you have in common with the other person that you never noticed before. You might both have jobs that you love or your favorite city is Berlin. And I'll bet that the next time you see this individual, those shared traits will be a lot more obvious to you.

I spent most of my life thinking that my dad and I were radically different when it came to our interests. We lost a lot of valuable time together as a result. But I could have just as easily focused on our similarities. He's also a huge music fan, for example. In fact, as one of his retirement projects, he recently wrote a novel about jazz musicians in the 1920s (which means we are also both authors too; there's another similarity).

Once you start actively looking at people you consider different from yourself, you'll notice a whole host of common traits that were staring you in the face all along. Do this often enough, and with enough people, and these mental grooves will get worn deeper and deeper, until seeing commonalities becomes second nature.

## Identify Points of Agreement

Common ground is precious in persuasive interactions. In fact, shared beliefs should be front and center. If you see a discussion headed toward conflict, emphasizing the common ground is a great way to combat your own tendencies, while also setting the stage for persuasion.

By flagging these points of agreement and giving them prime billing, you're not only changing your own outlook; you're making it clear to the other person that, for the most part, the two of you are on the same page about what needs to happen—you're just haggling over the details. At that point, the conversation is no longer a winner-take-all grudge match but a conversation about how to reach a goal that both of you see as valuable. That leaves you very well placed to influence the other person's views on the subject.

 **RECAP**

Human beings have a lot more similarities than we do differences—we're just not very good at remembering this.

An outlook that emphasizes our similarities can enable you to find common ground with whomever you're talking to, and give your audience the sense that you're already on their side.

People who are skilled at seeing commonalities instead of differences also find it easier to relate to people of different backgrounds, experiences, ages, and seniority.

Adopting a commonality-based point of view is easy, so long as you're willing to make the effort. That process begins with these techniques:

1. Make the choice to emphasize similarities.
2. Practice seeing shared traits.
3. Call out points of agreement.

If your default position is to see other people as more or less the same as you, that will help bring people to your side.

After all, we are all only 0.1 percent different.

## PRINCIPLE 3: EMPATHETIC

Soulful persuasion usually involves engaging with people who disagree with you. To do this effectively, you need to be able to assess situations from alternative perspectives and understand why people hold views different from yours. You need to be empathetic.

There are three essential habits that add up to the kind of empathetic character that will benefit you as a persuader.

### Make It About Them

Truly empathetic people have developed a natural curiosity about those around them. They initiate incisive conversations about topics that are relevant and meaningful to their conversation partners. They seek out and acquire knowledge about different cultures and ways of life in order to understand others more deeply. And they listen and learn far more than they judge. As a result, when it comes time to wield influence, they can draw on a highly textured and accurate picture of how others see the world.

### Seek Out Collaborations

Empathetic people are also eager to team up with others to achieve common aims, whether at work, in their community, in their family, or among their friends. They find value in joining forces with people from diverse backgrounds and areas of expertise. For this reason, others are more likely to see them as fellow team members—a perception that is perhaps more important than any other when it comes to changing minds.

## See Commonalities, Not Differences

Finally, the kind of empathy I've described requires a mindset that emphasizes our common humanity. People have far more in common than we have separating us. And when we place too much emphasis on our distinct races, genders, levels of wealth and education, or affinity groups, we are contributing to losing the common ground and driving a wedge between people that makes persuasion challenging.

Approaching each individual as an equal will make you more approachable, and enable you to talk to nearly anyone. It will also encourage others to return the favor, leaving you well placed to persuade.

Understand them and they will understand you.

PRINCIPLE 4

SOULFUL

Soul-
f u l -
ness    is
about    a
deep,  emo-
tional  connec-
tion   to   things
more  fundamental
than   our   everyday
concerns about money,
pleasure,    status,   and
identity.
Soulfulness  is  a  commitment  to  personal  values  and
principles.
My attempt to make my efforts
more soulful—more true to something
eternal and universal—has been a major
aspect of my career. Mekanism prides itself on advancing the "soul and science of
storytelling." We tell stories that display not
only a high level of technical skill but also an
emotional sensitivity to what matters most to all of
us at the core.
If you can live in a way that is animated by something more elevated than the practical and immediate,
influence will flow.

Chapter 10

# the importance of skill-hunting

*It is possible to fly without motors but not without knowledge and skill.*

—Wilbur Wright

The most powerful kind of persuasiveness is one that flows from a well-formed character. When you've worked to develop certain personal traits and skills, people will take notice.

Some of the habits and dispositions I've discussed—including respectfulness, positivity, and generosity—mostly pertain to your interactions with other people. But your character isn't just revealed in the ways you negotiate the social world. It's also evident in your approach to work and your interests.

By work, I don't just mean the things people pay you money to do, although that certainly is part of it. I'm referring to something much broader: any task or project you set yourself, regardless of the context. This includes everything from cooking dinner to planning a trip, learning a musical instrument, or getting it done at the office.

What does your home-cooking technique or your violin chops have to do with persuasion? Well, if persuasion is about character, and your relationship to work is a window into your character, then quite a lot. This isn't hard to see. The person who habitually cuts corners and settles for "good enough" in most things is never going to be very influential. In fact, "Who cares what he thinks?" would be a common response to such an individual.

Now think of the professional athlete, celebrity chef, musician, or some other elite, highly skilled individual. Such people don't just wield influence; they wield it in domains far beyond their own area of expertise. When they express a political opinion, it can be national news. When they recommend a book, endorse a sneaker, or boycott a brand, they can move markets. They've earned that clout by displaying the focus and intensity required to excel at something difficult. That's why Bono gets to hang out with the Dalai Lama and why Robert Downey Jr. meets with the Queen of England.

Remarkably, the persuasiveness of such highly accomplished individuals has little to do with what we know about them personally. Oftentimes we have no way of judging how informed they are or how sound their judgment is or how honest they are. Instead, their influence flows from their relationship to their skill.

Thankfully, persuasiveness of this kind doesn't require world-class mastery of a given skill. It simply demands a serious, rigorous, skill-based approach to whatever tasks and projects you choose to pursue. In other words, it requires a concern for doing things well and properly—not just getting them done as quickly, cheaply, and efficiently as possible. It's an approach I call "skill-hunting." And by adopting a skill-hunting work ethic—and avoiding cheap work-arounds and relying solely on life hacks—you will end up displaying the kind of character that carries influence.

## Skillful People Are More Persuasive

When someone brings a level of proficiency or an aspiration for proficiency to their pursuits, it tends to show through in all kinds of small ways. And often it doesn't take an expert to recognize when someone is skillful. For instance, you can tell a skilled skier just by the way she stands on the hill, before she even pushes over her poles. And I don't know that much about dance, but I can tell when someone is a great dancer. It's what we mean when we say someone "looks like they know what they're doing." By the same token, most of us can tell on an instinctive level when someone is phoning it in or bullshitting that they know more than they do.

These assessments of someone's proficiency and seriousness also inform our sense of who they are as a person. It's why, when we press someone to perform to the fullest extent of their abilities, we often use the phrase "Show us what you're made of." When we engage skillfully with the world around us, we are baring our souls.

Moreover, the perception of someone as competent and well trained in some area lends them a general air of authority. People who habitually take the time to do things with skill and attention are easier to trust, and their opinions matter more to us. This is one of the reasons that celebrity endorsements are such a tried-and-true technique in my industry. When LeBron James or Justin Timberlake or Taylor Swift endorses a product, it carries a lot of weight and can have a significant effect on the public's behavior. It's why our It's On Us campaign launched by enlisting the help of famous faces likely to change minds about rape culture on college campuses. It's why Pepsi built a campaign around Beyoncé. And why Michael Jordan is still helping to sell sneakers sixteen years after he stopped playing ball. Skill never goes out of style.

The power of celebrity endorsements is well documented. For instance, a recent study by Anita Elberse of Harvard Business School and Jeroen Verleun of Barclays Capital found that athlete endorsements drive up brand sales by an average of 4 percent. And when an athlete notches a major accomplishment, it tends to boost sales of the products they endorse.[1]

Why does this work? In part it's because celebrities are familiar faces, sure. But it's also because these individuals are the best at what they do. They bring an unrivaled level of excellence and skill to their work. And the fact that they hold themselves to such high standards adds gravity to their opinion—and gives the rest of us a good reason to follow their lead.

Most celebrities who are at the top of their professions have also devoted themselves to something greater than just financial success. You would never put in the time to become an elite athlete, actor, or chef if you didn't value doing great work for its own sake. There are easier and safer ways to get rich, after all. And that connection to something deep and eternal—what I mean by *soulfulness*—has a magnetic quality that contributes enormously to a person's persuasiveness.

Consider a recent survey that asked Americans to name the

most trusted people in the country. At the top of the list was Tom Hanks. When you think about it, that's a pretty strange finding. Most people have never met Hanks, and they never will. On top of that, they have no real evidence that he is, say, a clear thinker, a reliable source of facts, or even a well-intentioned person. For all we know, he could be a compulsive liar.

People who trust him aren't basing their confidence in Hanks on anything rational. Their sense of trust is the result of one thing—that Hanks is an incredibly skilled actor.[2] He may have made some bad movies in his career, and he'll likely make a few more in the future. But he's rarely, if ever, given an artless performance, or just phoned it in, or bullshitted his way through a role. He's someone who executes his job with extraordinary proficiency and seriousness.

The same can be said for the other celebrities among the list's top ten—including Meryl Streep and Maya Angelou. They too worked to become among the most skilled practitioners in their profession. And that skill has translated into influence.

Or just look at the recent career turn of former world chess champion Garry Kasparov. In his early forties, after holding the championship title for two decades, Kasparov retired from chess and became one of the world's most forceful advocates for human rights, free speech, and democracy—as well as one of Vladimir Putin's most vocal adversaries. He even ran for president of Russia in 2007. This from a man who spent most of his life studying a board game.

What made him great at chess was something that only his fellow grandmasters could really appreciate. But for everyone else, the very fact that he had mastered something difficult and complicated through years of hard work said something about his character. People listen to him. They pay attention.

Similarly, back in 2016, when Colin Kaepernick insisted on taking a knee during the national anthem to raise awareness of racial inequality in our country, it sparked a national conversation about police brutality and criminal justice reform, among other things. Had he not been among the best in the world at what he did, few would have cared if he engaged in this small act of nonviolent protest. The fact that he is so skilled and was playing at such a high level gave his actions and beliefs enormous gravity. As a result, his protest became a national story that almost every American knew about.

In a different way, the reason I'm more willing to believe a report in the *New York Times* or the *Wall Street Journal* than something I heard from a blogger or Twitter pundit is that I know that the journalists at these outlets place a high value on doing their jobs well. They have worked for years to develop their skills tracking down reputable sources, reporting facts clearly and accurately, honing their judgment, and writing with skill and exactitude. If one of these publications tells me some topic or incident is worth knowing about, I pay more attention.

Now, most of us will never be LeBron James, Tom Hanks, or Adele. But the outsized influence of figures such as these is proof of the connection between work ethic and persuasion. And just because most of us will never play in the NBA or win an Academy Award doesn't mean we can't all bring a level of proficiency and seriousness to what we do.

When you take the time to attack activities with skill and constantly strive to improve, others can tell. And in most situations, that unmistakable competence makes people a lot more willing to trust you and take your views to heart.

This is what I mean by skill-hunting: *an approach to work that aims at proficiency and improvement.*

Unfortunately, the whole idea of skill-hunting is anathema to many of today's most popular approaches to work. Just look at the rise of life-hacking. This philosophy involves adopting the right shortcuts to boost productivity with minimal effort. Everywhere you look, people are dispensing advice on how to maximize your efficiency by cutting out unnecessary work. This might involve using prewritten email templates to blast through your inbox, or listening to books on tape while you eat your morning oatmeal, or adopting a faster method for folding your laundry. Some of these can really come in handy, no doubt about it. And sometimes minimizing the amount of time you spend on mundane work will clear the space required for the more meaningful, skill-based activities.

For instance, my good friend Tim Ferriss is a master at enhancing his efficiency in ways that make life more fulfilling. In fact, he's a prime example of the kind of skill-hunting mindset I'm advocating. More than anyone else I know, Tim excels at breaking down complex skills in ways that enable him to master them quickly and deeply—whether it's cooking, speaking a foreign language, dancing, or Chinese kickboxing.[3] He is on a constant skill hunt, and his insights and achievements continue to be a huge inspiration.

Life-hacking is something different. The word "hack" comes from the tech world, where, according to one definition, it means "an inelegant solution to a problem. In this sense, a hack gets the job done but in an inefficient, un-optimal or ugly way."[4] A hack might be good for the time being. And it might even save your butt when you're in a jam. But I don't think it's a way to live.

At the extreme, the whole idea behind this philosophy is that every second of your waking life should be used as efficiently as possible. We are more than just worker bees—we are people with passions and values and purposes and soul. And substituting for these sources of meaning with something as cold and mechanical as efficiency or productivity is soulless. Whom would you rather trust: the person who is always looking for a nifty shortcut, or the person who doesn't mind putting in a little extra work when the situation requires it?

On the other end of the spectrum, there are plenty of business advice gurus who will tell you that if you want to get your startup off the ground, the only real secret is to put in as much time and work as you can manage—to live the pain. This can also be tied to what Malcolm Gladwell refers to as the ten-thousand-hour rule: that it takes ten thousand hours of doing any activity to master it (that's about ninety minutes a day for twenty years). Tim Ferris would argue that even if the data says ten thousand hours for most people, most people learn things the wrong way—or, as he would imply, the *long* way. Ferriss argues that quality of practice far outweighs quantity of practice.

Again, there's some truth to both ways of thinking. Without hours of practice, you'll never be great at anything. And yes, launching a business requires a huge time commitment. But focusing purely on time is a mistake. Just because you're working long hours doesn't mean you're getting closer to your goal. In fact, sometimes coming in early and burning the midnight oil is a complete waste of time, if you don't spend that time well.

For new entrepreneurs, meanwhile, it's common to feel that if you aren't busy all the time, you're doing something wrong. This can lead to a compulsion to work as much as possible—not in order to achieve success but simply to stay busy. Entrepreneur and writer Nat Eliason calls this kind of attitude "struggle porn," a phenomenon he describes as "a masochistic obsession with pushing yourself harder, listening to people tell you to work harder, and broadcasting how hard you're working." He points out that it can have some really horrible consequences. It can lead business owners to waste a fortune keeping their venture going long after it's proven to be a failure. They mistake their hard work for success and progress, even though their company isn't going to go anywhere.[5] They think if they just work harder, it will come together. But it won't. Worshipping work for the sake of work is a mistake.

The person who spends every available hour solely focused on growing their business, or just maximizing their wealth, isn't someone you're likely to find very trustworthy. With individuals like this, it's easy to get the sense that they're only looking out for themselves, and that they'd gladly sell you down the river if it got them a touch closer to just another milestone.

And then there's the person who works long hours as a way of signaling their value and status to those around them. They never miss an opportunity to take on a new project, and they seem to take a perverse joy in expressing how stressed, sleep-deprived, and overscheduled they are. For these sorts of people, busyness itself can seem like its own reward—so long as everyone around them knows how busy they are.

If you work in an office, you've likely encountered this last person often. Whatever you might think of such individuals, they aren't exactly persuasive. In fact, they tend to infect others with stress and insecurity, driving people away instead of drawing them in.

Skill-hunting falls between these two extremes. It strikes a healthy middle ground. Your goal should be to avoid all of these traps by developing a balanced approach to work that aims at doing things well and proficiently. Not overdoing it to the point of monomaniacal obsession or "struggle porn" masochism, but also not always looking for the shortcut. And the first step to doing that is adopting a skill-based mindset.

## Shift to Skill-Hunting

Whereas a task-based mindset focuses on just getting things crossed off, regardless of the process, a skill-hunting mindset values process as much as the finished product.

The difference between task-based and skill-based approaches is the difference between learning a single great recipe, on the one hand, and studying the fundamentals of cooking, on the other; between cramming for an exam and mastering an area of knowledge; between counting calories and adopting a healthy, balanced diet.

In fact, the concept of skill-hunting goes to the heart of soulful persuasion. This approach eschews tricks and shortcuts (task-based strategies) in favor of persuasion that results from deeply imbedded habits and character traits (skills). Once you embrace a skill-hunting outlook, it will change the way you attack all kinds of projects. You'll stop focusing solely on results and start seeing activities in terms of the skills required to perform them well.

Say you're interested in losing a few pounds in anticipation of a beach trip you have coming up. From this perspective, your goal is to look a certain way, and the path toward achieving that goal is irrelevant. If you shift to a skill-based mindset, it changes the entire nature of the project. The question is no longer "What's the easiest way to lose weight?" but "What do I need to do to get fit?" Getting fit is something that requires skills—the skills, for instance, of understanding how your body reacts to food and exercise, of incorporating physical activity into your everyday life, of preparing and eating nutritious foods, and of exercising with good form. Fitness itself is the body's skill at functioning properly.

If you approach the project in this way, you won't just look better in time for Maui—you'll be healthier, fitter, and stronger. You'll have acquired abilities that you can then apply in all kinds of other situations. There might have been faster ways to lose weight, but you'll never regret putting in the extra time to achieve improvements that run deep and carry benefits more substantial than having a great beach body.

Let's say your boss gives you a project that requires you to use new software that you're not very proficient with. You could pass that part of the project off to your colleague, who is an expert with that program (which I would most certainly do). But you could also see the situation as an opportunity to develop a new skill. This might mean coming in early to watch YouTube tutorials about the software, or taking some work home with you over the weekend so that you can learn through trial and error. Again, this isn't the most direct way of getting the job done. But in the end you'll have developed a new skill—one that may come in handy in ways you couldn't have anticipated.

The more you come to rely on skills for the right projects, and not hacks or work-arounds or working yourself to the bone, the more these skillful activities will become second nature. As this happens, you'll no longer have to rely on conscious procedures but will be able to act instinctively, using your unconscious judgment to guide your behavior.

Think about it: Once the piano player puts in years of practice to learn to play her instrument skillfully, she can let the music flow from her without thinking. The technical aspects of her performance become automatic. That's about as efficient as it gets. But it's the kind of efficiency that doesn't come at the cost of high quality.

Just as important, someone who attacks projects from a skill-based mindset is displaying a certain character. They are showing themselves to be the kind of person who values doing things properly, even if it means putting in extra time and effort. This kind of character makes you inherently trustworthy and influential.

## How, Not Just What

At its simplest, the skill-based mindset is about valuing the way something is done just as much as the end results. It's about *how* just as much as *what*. And the persuasive benefits of this kind of thinking don't just apply to people. In fact, in recent years, brands have recognized that their influence with consumers depends a lot on the way they do business—not merely on whether they deliver a solid product or service.

This explains the recent explosion in the market for products that are ethically made, sustainable, and sourced through fairtrade policies. Patagonia, for instance, summarizes its mission this way: "Build the best product, cause no unnecessary harm, use business to inspire and implement solutions to the environmental crisis."[6] Apple, meanwhile, has made a big deal out of manufacturing its latest computers out of 100 percent recycled aluminum, and powering its business entirely with renewable energy sources.[7]

Even Walmart, a company that to many is the embodiment

of bottom-dollar efficiency, is placing more emphasis on how they do things. The brand has set aggressive goals for reducing greenhouse gas emissions, cutting waste in their operations, and sourcing products responsibly.[8]

What these brands have realized is that how they do business matters just as much to consumers' buying decisions as what they are selling. Sure, there might be a cheaper, faster, and more efficient way to make a certain product. But by showing a willingness to do things properly, a growing number of brands are revealing something about their character that they know consumers will respond to.

## The Art of Living Skillfully

So how does one go about practicing this skill-hunting approach to work? After all, there are only so many hours in a day. And unless you're Leonardo da Vinci, becoming a master in everything you do isn't a realistic goal. Fortunately, the kind of skillful living I'm advocating doesn't require you to become a virtuoso at everything—just that you attack projects with the goal of acquiring and improving your skills. You might only ever be a so-so violinist or a passable cook. But as long as you seek to get more proficient at these skills every time you engage in them, you'll have successfully embraced the skill-based outlook.

If something is worth doing, it's worth doing well. And what counts as "well" can only be learned by diving in and engaging in the activity with focus and intent—instead of trying to get it over with.

There are several important strategies to put this idea into action.

## Deliberate Practice

Perhaps the most essential part of acquiring any skill is learning to engage in what the psychologist Anders Ericsson calls "deliberate practice." This is a kind of focused, systematic practice that is designed to push you out of your comfort zone. It's the opposite of rote repetition or just "fooling around."

Picking up a guitar and mindlessly jamming isn't deliberate practice. Focusing all of your attention on a specific lick that's just out of reach, noticing where it goes wrong, and consciously correcting—that's deliberate practice.[9]

A big part of deliberate practice is knowing when to stop. Since this kind of practice requires a high level of energy and focus, it's actually better to do it in small bursts. If you stay at it for too long a stretch, fatigue can set in, and you start to get sloppy. So attempting to log as many hours as possible in the shortest amount of time is a mistake. Rather, aim to practice as intently as you can for as long as possible. When you feel your focus slipping, you stop.

## The Two-Year Skill Hunt

This one is pretty straightforward. If you want to live a life defined by proficiency, you need to keep learning. And one way to do that is by picking up a major new skill every other year. Doesn't matter if it's photography, surfing, or knitting. What matters is that you're genuinely motivated to learn it—not master it, but learn it.

Again, Tim Ferriss is a great example here. He has turned the regular acquisition of new skills into a way of life. And it's the main reason he has such a devoted following. Even people who don't always agree with him still take him very seriously. And it's because he shows a high level of seriousness in everything he does.

If you do this for long enough, and with enough activities, you'll become familiar with the patterns of acquiring a new skill, which in turn will make you better at learning and help you become a more skillful person in many different areas of your life.

The biggest difficulty to get over is the period at the beginning where you will totally suck. If you get in the habit of learning new skills regularly, you'll come to see that the seemingly hopeless early days are just an inevitable part of the process, and nothing to get frustrated over.

## My "Sweet Science" Experiment

My own recent adventures in the boxing ring provide a useful example of the benefits that can come from regularly acquiring new skills. I got interested in the sport almost two years ago, and I expected to pick it up somewhat quickly. How hard could it be? After all, there are only about six punches to master—the jab, the cross, left and right hook, left and right uppercut.

I got the hang of the technique after just a few months of working with a trainer. And I went into my first sparring match with a lot of confidence and what I thought was a sound strategy. But, as Mike Tyson once said, "everybody has a plan until they get punched in the mouth."[10]

In my case, fear of getting punched wasn't really an issue. In fact, I had the opposite problem. I didn't mind getting hit as much as most people did. But I tended to rush in toward my opponent too quickly. I was a swarmer boxer, but without the skills part. This caused me to smother my punches—to get too close to effectively hit my opponent. As a result, I left myself vulnerable. And usually by the third round or so, I had taken far more punches than I had given.

My mistake was that I leaned too heavily on my innate strength (my willingness to get hit) instead of taking the time to work on key techniques that didn't come naturally to me (like footwork and slipping punches). I thought I'd found the path of least resistance. This was a pretty painful way to learn the value of doing things the right way.

These days, I train and work with my coach, perfecting my punches, my blocking, my footwork—in other words, focusing on the fundamentals and the skills. I've gotten a lot better on technique. I find it easier to exercise good form and stay in control mentally, even when I get agitated while sparring. As the core skills I'm learning become more and more like second nature, I'm also improving at improvising and reacting to unexpected developments. I've come to judge each session on whether or not I honed my skills. And this is going to take many more years of work.

What I've found is that the wisdom I've picked up by engaging in this sort of deliberate practice for boxing is applicable to learning a skill in a totally different area. For instance, boxing has taught me how to stay disciplined even when I'm in pain and uncomfortable; how to not get discouraged when something doesn't come naturally; and how advice that might seem stupid or old-fashioned when you first hear it can turn out to be indispensable once you have a little experience under your belt. These lessons don't just apply to boxing—they apply to everything.

There is no growth in comfort.

## Passions, Not Hobbies

If there's a hobby you spend a lot of time on already, stop thinking of it as a fun diversion and attempt to start thinking of it as
a passion—a domain of skill or knowledge that you value for its
own sake and strive to get better at. Instead of using this activity
to pass time pleasantly, treat it as a pursuit that demands deliberate practice.

Maybe you like playing pickup basketball at the park every
weekend, but you rarely put in any time working on your free
throw or getting better at burying threes. All it takes is an extra
thirty minutes of deliberate practice before or after your next
pickup game to turn this easy pastime into a bona fide skill.
If you play poker once a month with friends and love it, stop
thinking of it as an occasional social activity and put in some
time to study strategy, seek out advice from better players, and
raise your own level of performance each time you play. Maybe
even see if you can learn to count cards.

Similarly, if you're a casual fan of a specific band or a film
director, do the work to become an expert. Read whatever criticism you can get your hands on, and seek out obscure works
you've never encountered before. In this way, you'll be turning
your casual enjoyment into skillful engagement—which is always more satisfying.

## Quality over Quantity

It's a cliché, I know, but it happens to be true: it's better to do a
few things proficiently than to be terrible at a long list of things.
In practice, this means avoiding tasks that you don't have the

time to carry out with skill and focus, or which don't contribute to your improvement in any real way. This isn't always possible.

For instance, many people feel compelled to volunteer for projects or engage in minor tasks at work even though these activities aren't essential to their actual job. As a result, their attention gets divided into smaller and smaller segments, diluting the overall quality of the work they perform, and preventing them from improving at the skills that really matter to them.

Instead, get comfortable saying no to things that aren't essential to your larger goals, whether professionally or personally. This might mean choosing not to be the fourteenth person in a meeting that isn't really relevant to your current projects, or not chiming in on every email chain that appears in your inbox. Use that extra time to execute your real work with focus, care, and skill.

## Straight Facts

When it comes to persuasion, one of the most important abilities you can develop is that of handling facts skillfully and responsibly. People who are known for getting their facts right, and who excel at sorting good information from bad, are just more trustworthy and, as a result, more influential. When they speak, people listen, because what they're saying is probably true.

By contrast, someone who is careless with facts is inherently unreliable, almost by definition. It's no coincidence that when defense attorneys are trying to undermine a witness's story, they look for small inaccuracies in that person's testimony. By doing this, these lawyers are trying to portray the witness as someone who lacks a proper respect for factual accuracy and thus isn't worth listening to.

Learning to treat facts with a high level of respect requires conscious practice. Specifically, it requires a kind of learned vigilance that treats most information as suspect until you yourself have checked it out. Being conscientious about factual information also means developing the skills of a good researcher. If you're going to cite a statistic or point to a historical example in conversation, be sure you've done the work to determine if what you're saying is truly accurate.

Even slipping up on a seemingly trivial matter of fact can have serious repercussions for your reputation and, thus, your persuasiveness. Simply because a piece of information isn't important to you doesn't mean it's not important to your audience. And if someone in your audience is better informed than you on a certain topic and notices when you get big things slightly wrong, he or she will quickly form an impression of you as someone who plays fast and loose with the truth. That impression puts you at a huge disadvantage if your goal is to persuade.

Most of the time, this due diligence won't be noticeable—it will remain entirely behind the scenes. But the one time out of ten someone challenges you in a meeting, or asks a surprising question, you'll be ready with the details. You will have developed a well-earned reputation as someone who knows what they're talking about.

 ## RECAP

We gravitate toward people who are great at what they do. We trust them, seek their advice, and follow their lead. When they express an opinion, we take it seriously. That's because when you value high quality and attack your activities with skill and

focus, it reveals something about your character that, once ob-
served, subconsciously lends you tremendous influence in the
eyes of others.

It follows, then, that from the standpoint of persuasion, the
best way to approach any project, large or small, is to see it in
terms of the skills required to perform it well—and to commit
to developing and improving those skills. This is skill-hunting
in a nutshell. And it strikes an important balance between life-
hacking and the masochistic "more is more is more" work philosophy that many blindly subscribe to.

You can make the shift to this skill-based approach by:

1. Deliberate practice
2. The two-year skill hunt
3. Passions, not hobbies
4. Quality over quantity
5. Straight facts

Over time, the high standards and commitment to quality
you display will come to define you in the eyes of others.

If you can achieve that, not only skill but influence will
follow.

Chapter 11

# personal jesus

---

*If my mind can conceive it, and my heart can believe it,
then I can achieve it.*

—Muhammad Ali

Persuasion is the art of influencing people's actions and
beliefs. There are plenty of ways to go about this: you can intimidate people, pay them off, scare them, appeal to their self-
interest, or guilt them. But there is no better motivator in the
world than inspiration.

When we feel inspired to accomplish a goal or take a position,
we aren't merely motivated, but motivated in a life-affirming,
pleasurable, energizing way. Inspiration fills us with a sense of
possibility and gives us the determination to push ourselves beyond our normal limits. It moves us to be better than we are. It
feeds the soul.

When you look closely, many of the projects we take up in life had their start in a moment of inspiration. The reason I learned to play a musical instrument was the feeling I had after listening to the bass riffs in Joy Division's "Love Will Tear Us Apart." Simple. Memorable. Beautiful to me. I went into advertising not because of any practical considerations but because, as a kid, I loved "Oh, yeah!" from the Kool-Aid character—the anthropomorphic pitcher with a smile on his face that busted through walls and ruined your goddamn house. Kids would yell, "Hey, Kool-Aid," and he would show up with his red sugar water. I wanted to be a part of that magic of ruining people's houses with cartoons.

And when someone inspirational asks us to do something, it's pretty easy to say yes. If Jon Stewart appeared in my office right now and asked to borrow my car, I'd throw him the keys.

Striving to be inspirational in your daily life is one of the most powerful strategies for becoming a more persuasive person. There is no single path to becoming inspirational—as evidenced by the great diversity of people you are inspired by. And in a sense, every habit and character trait discussed in this book will help you to become more inspirational. If you do the work to be more generous, more respectful, and more skilled at telling stories, you will have a character that many are sure to draw inspiration from. But inspiring others is also about living a life of principles, moving others to challenge their preconceptions of what's possible, and even doing some good in the world.

Being inspirational does not mean you never make mistakes. We are all human, after all. It just means that you are always aiming to try your best to live according to your personal principles.

## How Inspiration Really Works

When I think of the most inspirational figures in history, whether Harriet Tubman or Albert Einstein, one feature stands out: they all displayed extraordinary principle and integrity. That is, they were willing to put their beliefs into action, even when doing so wasn't popular and meant risking their own immediate interests. And in so doing, they were able to change the way people around them thought and acted.

As a boxer, Muhammad Ali was a marvel to behold—a superhuman combination of brilliant technique, timing, speed, accuracy, and raw talent. But the real reason he inspires has to do with the time he spent outside the ring in the late 1960s and early 1970s. In 1966, two years after winning the heavyweight championship at the age of twenty-two, Ali refused to be drafted to fight in the war in Vietnam. He objected both for religious reasons—he was a practicing Muslim—and because he saw the war itself as unjust on his own moral grounds.

In the years that followed, he was convicted of dodging the draft and sentenced to five years in prison. Half of the country saw him not as the principled conscientious objector he was but as a coward. Although he remained free while his conviction was appealed, he had his boxing license revoked in every single state. He lost his passport, which prevented him from fighting outside the country. And he was stripped of his heavyweight title.

The fortitude it took for Ali to stand up the way he did is amazing. This was a man at the height of his powers as a boxer being denied the right to practice his profession. He could have submitted, played nice, and done what the authorities wanted him to do—if not for himself, then for his family. But he didn't.

Instead, he watched his athletic prime pass him by while he waited for his appeal to wind its way through the sluggish court system. It wasn't until 1971 that the Supreme Court finally overturned his conviction in a unanimous vote.[1] He had been out of boxing for four years.

And it took until 1974, when he was thirty-two (pretty old for a boxer in the 1970s, especially one who relied on speed and agility as much as Ali), for him to win back the heavyweight title in his historic fight against twenty-five-year-old George Foreman in Kinshasa, Zaire.[2] Who knows what he could have accomplished as a fighter had he been allowed to ply his trade during his mid- to late-twenties.

Ali stuck to his principles not just when it was easy but even when he knew full well that it could cost him his livelihood and even his freedom. He stated repeatedly that he was willing to go to jail if that was what the courts decided. He scratched by for years with almost no money to his name. And instead of fleeing secretly to a foreign country, he remained in the public eye, speaking his mind and inspiring others to have the courage of their convictions. As it turned out, history would be on Ali's side, but at the time much of the country did not value Ali speaking his mind.

Had he given in and said what he had to in order to keep his boxing license and stay out of jail, few reasonable people would have blamed him. We would have thought, "I'd probably do the same thing in his position." That he stuck by his principles raised the standards for everybody else. Because of Ali, the rest of the world had one less excuse to take the easy route when our values were challenged. Compromising our principles got just a little bit harder.

This is what inspirational figures can accomplish. People like this can push us past our natural limits, and give us the strength and motivation to do better. They can persuade us to be our most purposeful selves.

## Breaking the Bystander Spell

This kind of commitment to principle can be extraordinarily effective at influencing people's behavior. And in many situations, all it takes is one individual to inspire a wave of change and break people from what psychologists call the *bystander effect*.

The bystander effect was first explored by psychologists John M. Darley and Bibb Latané in the late 1960s. That research came about in response to the 1964 murder of twenty-eight-year-old Kitty Genovese in Queens, New York. Genovese was brutally raped and stabbed to death in the street in front of her apartment one night. At the time, it was widely reported that dozens of people admitted that they had either seen the event or heard it happen, but failed to stop the attack or even call the police.[3]

That account turned out to be exaggerated. Two people actually did call the police. But the false version of the story captured the nation's attention and sparked a conversation around one question: Why did nobody intervene?

That was the question that Darley and Latané took up in their landmark experiments. They hypothesized that the more people who witness a crisis, the less likely it is that any one of them will step forward and do something about it. And that's exactly what their research demonstrated.

In one experiment, an undergraduate student is invited to participate in a discussion about personal problems and life at college. During the conversation, another participant, who is in fact part of the experiment, pretends to have some sort of seizure. The point of the exercise was to see whether the first student would help the seizure victim, and if so, how long it would take. More than that, the study looked at how those responses changed depending on how many people were on the scene.

Sure enough, students were far more likely to help—and to do so quickly—when there was nobody else witnessing the seizure. The larger the group of witnesses got, the less likely students were to intervene. Those that did try to help, meanwhile, waited longer when the group was larger.[4]

In other words, when we're in a crowd, it's a lot easier for all of us to sit on our hands—to be bystanders—in situations that call for action. This is true even when failing to act means violating our most commonsense ethical principles, like "When someone is in trouble, you should help them."

One possible cause of the bystander effect, according to Darley and Latané, is what's known as the *diffusion of responsibility*. When there are plenty of other people around, we feel that our own obligation to help is somehow less potent, which makes us more willing to sit back and do nothing. Similarly, any blame for failing to take action is also diffused among the group.[5] "If nobody else is doing anything," we think, "why should I?"

These findings are damn depressing. But there is a silver lining to be found, and it's this: when one person stands up and acts, it makes it a whole lot harder for the rest of the crowd to remain bystanders. Seriously, all it takes is one person to break the spell of the diffusion of responsibility and make others feel compelled to lend a hand. And that's exactly the role played by inspirational people.

You can see this dynamic playing out all over the place if you look for it. For instance, if some down-on-his-luck individual is asking for money on the subway, sometimes our instinct is to avoid eye contact and refuse to part with our pocket change—until just one other person gives him a few bucks, or even a few cents. Then you'll often notice the floodgates open, as people reach for whatever money they can spare. This is also why charity telethons will keep a running tally of how much money other viewers have given. (These psychological tendencies can be gamed, of course. For instance, smart sidewalk musicians will often throw a bit of their own money into their hat before they start, to give the impression that people have already donated.)

Inspirational people don't dictate to us the right course of action. Nobody needs to tell us that it's right to give to people in need or protect the environment. Instead, those people move us to stand by principles that we already hold, and to resist our baser and more selfish tendencies, including our willingness to be bystanders.

That's exactly what happened in the 1950s when a black seamstress from Montgomery, Alabama, named Rosa Parks refused to go along with the city's segregation laws—and specifically the rule that required black people to sit at the back of the bus. The absurdity and inhumanity of those Jim Crow laws were plain for everybody to see. But it was rare that anybody stood up against them.

On Thursday, December 1, 1955, while riding the bus home from her job at the Montgomery Fair department store, Parks was asked to give up her seat for a white passenger. The request was made even more infuriating by the fact that Parks was already seated in the "colored" section of the bus. The "white" section had filled up. So in order to create more seats for the white passengers, the bus driver asked Parks and three others to stand. Parks was having none of it. And with a simple response,

"Not today," she refused to be a bystander. This is the most historically significant example of the power of no.

As she later explained, "People always say that I didn't give up my seat because I was tired, but that isn't true. I was not tired physically. . . . No, the only tired I was, was tired of giving in."[6]

Her extraordinary act of civil disobedience landed her in police custody. Days later, she was convicted of disorderly conduct, but she appealed the decision. Her arrest and trial inspired a large-scale boycott of the city's bus system that lasted over a year—a now-legendary protest led by none other than twenty-six-year-old Martin Luther King Jr. And her appeal eventually made it to the Supreme Court in 1956, which ruled in favor of Parks. That decision led to the desegregation of the Montgomery bus system and paved the way for the Civil Rights Act of 1964.[7] All of this because a single person pushed back against laws that violated her own sense of integrity, equality, and self-worth. She wasn't the only person who recognized these laws as a moral atrocity. But she was among the few people who refused to give in to the bystander effect. As a result, she helped reshape history.

Another of my favorite examples of this principle in action involves the green building pioneer David Gottfried. After working as a developer for years, Gottfried came to realize just how much environmental damage was caused by construction projects. He saw that the profession that was benefiting his wallet was also harming the planet. This was twenty-five years ago, back when a building's environmental impact was the last thing that developers and architects thought about when breaking ground on a new project. Perhaps more than any other person, Gottfried is the one who changed these norms—not just here in the United States but around the world. He took his skills and network and set about inspiring change.

In the 1990s, he cofounded two organizations: the U.S. Green Building Council and the World Green Building Council. Together, these groups have sparked a global movement aimed at preserving our planet through sustainable buildings. Most notably, Gottfried was the driving force behind the Leadership in Energy and Environmental Design (LEED) standards. This is a system for rating a building's environmental soundness based on a wide variety of factors, from the materials and resources used in construction to the building's energy and water efficiency and its effects on air quality and occupant health.

LEED certification is now a standard requirement for all kinds of construction projects around the planet. In fact, LEED-certified buildings can be found in 167 countries. And daily, an estimated 2.2 million square feet of real estate earns certification.[8] Compared to their alternative, LEED-certified buildings produce 34 percent less $CO_2$ pollution and consume 25 percent less energy.[9]

The consequences of this are hard to overstate. Many of the buildings we construct right now will be here for generations— which means the decisions we make today will have massive long-term consequences for the environment. Consider that buildings are responsible for roughly 40 percent of our nation's $CO_2$ emissions.[10] By ensuring that today's buildings use resources and energy efficiently and generate a minimum of pollution, we can make tremendous progress toward protecting our planet. That was the insight that motivated Gottfried.

The determination of this one person has already delivered world-changing benefits for our health and environment—and will continue to do so for centuries. As Gottfried once put it, "We are each the atom of change. If we can green ourselves and our sphere of influence, which are millions and billions of people, that can create the tidal wave of transformation that we need."[11] This shows that no matter your industry or profession, you can always figure out a way to do good based on skills, networks, and knowledge you already possess.

When nobody else is lending a hand or taking care of the environment, we can convince ourselves that it's okay to do nothing. But most of us know better, if only we are honest with ourselves. In our souls, we know full well when action is called for. And when just one person answers that call, it's harder for the rest of us to let ourselves off the hook. We think, "If this person can do it, what's my excuse?"

That's how inspirational people wield influence.

## Even an Ad Man Can Do Some Good

I thought of myself as a fairly principled person for much of my adult life. I had my beliefs, and I tried to stay informed about the world's most pressing problems. I supported candidates I genuinely believed in, and I had thoughtful conversations at parties about the state of our community and our country. I never did much about it—mainly because I thought that today's biggest challenges were too massive for someone like me to have any effect. You know, classic bystander thinking. But here's the thing: living a life of principle isn't the same as having insightful conversations. There is a huge gap between having an idea and following through with an idea. As they say, talk is cheap.

It was after partnering with Vice President Joe Biden on the It's On Us campaign that I realized this fact. Not coincidentally, that movement sought to combat the bystander effect by encouraging all Americans to step up and do their part to prevent sexual assault on campus. We recognized that what makes these horrible crimes possible is our reluctance to take responsibility, step away from the crowd, and prevent sexual assault before it happens.

In the years since that campaign I've taken this insight to the next level by cofounding an organization called the Creative Alliance. The idea was to tap into some of the world's most creative companies to help craft campaigns aimed at effecting real social change.

The Creative Alliance focuses on four key issues:

1. Anti-hate and discrimination
2. Gender equality
3. Educational access
4. Civic engagement

We started out with just nine partners four years ago. Today we have over ninety companies lending their talent and expertise to the organization—including powerhouses like CAA, Broadway Video, Comedy Central, MTV, and incredible advertising agencies like 72&Sunny, BBH, Subrosa, In Good Co, and Havas. We've been able to recruit these organizations in large part by breaking the spell of the bystander effect.

Our pitch to a lot of our partner companies is based entirely on inspiration: "We are willing to use our time, energy, resources, and expertise to promote real social good, instead of just selling products. Won't you join in and help lead a campaign that you care about?" When you tell someone they can use their powers for good, they light up.

To date, we've spearheaded over eight initiatives aimed at helping kids get to college, fighting discrimination, and promoting gender equality.[12] One of the Creative Alliance's most recent initiatives, #VoteTogether, aimed at increasing voter participation by hosting block parties, BBQs, and other events near polling places. We want to encourage individuals, families, and communities to see democratic participation as an opportunity to come together and celebrate—instead of as a source of divisiveness. We have some inspirational guiding principles as well: "Purpose over Profit," "Collaboration over Competition," and "Movements not Moments."

When building anything from scratch, creating inspiring founding principles is always useful in illuminating your path forward. If you had told me a few years ago that I could play even a small role in increasing educational attainment or fighting for gender equality, I wouldn't have believed you. I would have told you that people like me don't have time or skills to do things like that. That's a weak excuse that becomes a self-fulfilling prophecy. In fact, it turns out that people like me and you can do things like that, if only we make the simple decision to do so.

It's my way of refusing to be a bystander in the face of urgent social problems. And the unifying idea behind all of these initiatives is that each of us can do the same. We all have the power to leverage our skills to achieve something good—while earning a living.

## Swaying Through Personal Authority

One of the benefits of habitually striving to turn your values into action is that over time you earn a reputation for putting your money where your mouth is in ways that really matter. And that gives you personal authority.

When someone has this kind of authority, we tend to trust that their decisions are correct. Our natural impression of those with personal authority is that they are sincere, are well intentioned, and care about the right things. If this is how you are perceived by others, they will be highly inclined to follow your lead when you express an opinion.

Martin Luther King Jr. is the best example of this dynamic in action. It was because of his extraordinary authority—earned over years of leadership, scholarship, and devotion to social equality—that he was able to convince members of the civil rights movement to advance their cause *nonviolently*. There was plenty of temptation in that period to fight this political battle through violence. This was completely understandable, given the centuries-long history of subjugation that affects the African American community to this day. But King almost single-handedly persuaded the activists of his time to pursue their cause through nonviolent means—sometimes while they themselves endured brutal violence at the hands of their opponents. He accomplished this remarkable feat, not with arguments or propaganda or force, but by wielding his hard-earned authority.

The result was one of the most exceptional nonviolent political uprisings in the history of the world. The Montgomery bus boycott, the March on Washington, and the Selma-to-Montgomery march remain models of peaceful political activism that are emulated the world over.[13]

Again, this is a pretty lofty example of how inspiration can impart influence. But it's an example that each of us can apply in our own lives. When you develop a reputation for acting from principle and caring about what's right, people will be far more willing to follow your lead and take your opinion to heart.

## How to Be Inspirational

There is not any one way to inspire others around you. When someone succeeds at being inspirational, it always has a lot to do with the person's specific time and circumstances. But there are a number of things you can do to develop the sort of character that others are likely to be inspired by.

### Preach Less

It's all well and good to talk a good game about the issues of the day. It's also the easiest thing in the world to do, thanks in no small part to our amazingly sophisticated information technologies. Your Twitter feed on a given afternoon will hit you over the head with all kinds of high-octane opinions and beliefs, much of which is just empty posturing.

Putting your commitments into action is a whole lot harder, which is why you don't see it as often. But the people who truly inspire us are the ones who get up off their butts and do their part to turn their beliefs into reality, even in a small and incremental way.

That's what David Gottfried did with the LEED standards, and it's what I did by helping start Creative Alliance. But you don't need to start a movement and go so lofty in order to follow through on your principles. Turning your values into action can be as simple as tutoring a local kid in math. Do whatever it is that you care about. And you can start something by leaning into what skills you have developed in an area you are familiar with. This increases your likelihood of success.

Once this sort of engagement becomes part of who you are, your words will carry a lot more weight.

## Use Your Powers for Good

We're all good at something. And one way to act on your deepest beliefs is to figure out how to put your particular gifts to use toward a cause. Are you a talented writer? Then reach out to a nonprofit organization you believe in and offer to help them craft a compelling message. Are you an expert financial advisor? Then find a way to pass on your wisdom to less-advantaged members of your community who are having money problems. I'm an ad man—someone who sells beer and lip balm for a living. And even I was able to use my skills to effect social change.

Whatever it is you excel at, just make sure you're also doing something that uses those powers to improve the lives of others, and not just to serve your own interests and those of your employers. That's what my buddy Josh Coombes has done, and to profound effect. Until recently Josh worked as a hairdresser in a London salon. He had always felt enormous personal compassion for the city's homeless but considered himself helpless to do anything. How can a hairdresser make an impact with the homeless? Then, three years ago, he had a life-changing epiphany: What if he used his skills as a hairdresser to improve the lives of London's disadvantaged? He grabbed his backpack, headed out on the street, and spent an hour cutting the hair of one homeless man. His hope was that, by using his skills in this way, he could give a little extra confidence to the people who most needed it.

But what he soon learned was that the haircut was simply a vehicle for human connection, and one that was just as fulfilling for him as it was for those whose hair he was cutting. As he did this again and again, he came to see his haircuts as a chance to get to know people and share his own passions, fears, and anxieties. By the end of each haircut, both Josh and the other person felt different—a little more human, a little more understood, and a little less helpless. In fact, when he talks about it, he stresses that the experiences he shares with homeless people are as important for him as for them.

He started posting stories about what he was doing on Instagram—complete with before-and-after pictures of the cuts—under the hashtag #DoSomethingForNothing. That's when I found him. The whole idea of using your skills to improve the world is obviously something I feel strongly about, and I wanted to get to know Josh better. I also wanted to share what he was doing with the people at Mekanism. So I got in touch with Josh and invited him to speak at our agency's annual summit.

The summit is a very special event for the company. It's the only time each year when the staff from all four of our offices gather in one place. We see it as an opportunity to step back from our day-to-day work, recharge our batteries, focus on big-picture goals and values, and, most of all, to get inspired. It's hard to hear about what Josh is doing without feeling inspired. So I knew he'd be a perfect addition to the festivities, which that year were in Mexico. Josh had never spoken at an event, but he loved the idea and quickly agreed to make the trip. He blew the doors off the place.

Since his early Instagram posts, Josh's efforts have transformed into a #DoSomethingForNothing movement that has inspired many others to follow his example. For instance, veterinarian Jade Statt has started an effort she calls StreetVet, which aims to help homeless people take better care of their dogs by providing everything from vaccinations to surgeries.[14] Meanwhile, photographer Tatjana Hoffman has founded There Is Hope Models, a modeling agency featuring London's homeless people, which aims to change the way the city's least advantaged are perceived—and how they perceive themselves.[15]

When people ask Josh how to get involved with #DoSomethingForNothing, his answer is simple: Write down three things you enjoy doing and are skilled at. Then write down three issues you're passionate about. "When you have them next to each other and you take a look at them for a while," he says, "you'll easily find ways to join those dots."

What Josh's example shows is that you don't need to change the course of history in order to improve people's lives right now. You just need to give something valuable away to someone in need. Even something as seemingly trivial as a haircut can be life-affirming.

Using your powers, whatever they might be, for good is the most direct route to personal integrity and purpose. By integrity, I mean the kind of personal harmony that comes when your abilities, actions, values, and goals all line up.

## Find Your Cause

Choosing a cause that's worth your time and energy can be a daunting task. Since I've gotten involved in social activism, I've been blown away by the number of amazing organizations—as well as lone activists—that are doing great work addressing problems. How do you decide where your energies should go?

Odds are, there's already an issue that you're passionate about, or at least a general topic that you strongly believe needs more attention than it's getting. Maybe it's criminal justice reform, or veterans' rights, or rare diseases. It could be a problem facing your local community, or even just your neighborhood. Start by doing some research and learning the nitty-gritty of whatever topic naturally draws you in. Once you've formed your own educated opinion about the topic, find organizations that are making progress in a way that hits home with you. Resources like GiveWell.org and Philanthropedia can be helpful guides in this phase of your research.

After you've whittled down your list to a few groups, dig into their written materials—research, annual reports, anything you can get your hands on. If their mission still speaks to you, call them up and talk to someone who is already involved. Most important, ask how you can lend a hand.

I'd also recommend limiting yourself to one or two main causes. Quality is more important than quantity. So focus on the activities and organizations where you're confident your contributions will have the biggest impact.

## Reach Out to Your Heroes

I'm amazed at how rarely it occurs to people to get in touch with the heroes who inspire them. We tend to think that those who accomplish great things are somehow superhuman—gifted with some special ability that we mere mortals lack. But this way of thinking can actually deter us from getting involved in the issues that matter to us.

Psychologists Penelope Lockwood and Ziva Kunda looked at the relationship between role models and inspiration. And what they've found is that while extraordinary people can be profound sources of motivation, they can also "lead to discouragement and self-deflation rather than the desired inspiration. This is likely to occur when the role model has achieved unattainable success at one's own domain of interest."[16] This makes sense. If it takes someone like Gandhi to effect real change in the world, what could someone like you or me hope to accomplish?

But adopting this attitude is a mistake. And one way to prevent this error is to reach out to those who inspire you. Send them an email, tweet at them, shoot them a DM, or go up to them after an event and introduce yourself. Start a conversation about your shared values. Ask questions about how they got where they are and what you can do to follow their example. And take them to coffee or lunch.

A lot of times these conversations won't go anywhere. You might not even get an email back. But you might also learn something, or even start a relationship that can last years. In those cases, you'll start to see these inspirational figures as not that very different from yourself in a lot of ways. As a result, the idea that their accomplishments are somehow beyond your reach will start to crumble. I am still friends with David Gottfried and Josh Coombes, and I reached out to them to get the relationship ball rolling.

You'll be surprised at how accessible our role models can be. Many of the individuals we hold in high regard love nothing more than to mentor people and pass on their knowledge. And because we get intimidated, you would be surprised at how few people actually reach out to them.

Over time, you'll develop a network of friends and conversation partners for whom doing good and personal integrity are a normal part of life. And this will help you hold yourself to similarly high standards.

 ## RECAP

Of all the ways of persuading another person to action, inspiration is without a doubt the most profound, and in a lot of cases the most powerful. If you can be a source of inspiration for others, you'll rarely struggle to have your opinions taken seriously. Your views will carry the weight of authority. And people will go out of their way to grant your requests. You will have achieved a kind of influence that goes far beyond salesmanship or rhetoric or bargaining. It is a persuasive power that comes directly from your soul.

Becoming a source of inspiration is a challenging, lifelong project. It involves constantly striving to act in accordance with your principles. Perhaps most important, inspirational figures have a highly developed capacity to resist the bystander effect and break away from the pack when their values demand action.

The most inspirational people:

1. Preach less and practice more
2. Use their powers for good
3. Seek out causes that advance their values
4. Reach out to their heroes

If you adopt these habits and make them part of your everyday life, you'll eventually become the kind of person who gives others a reason to act—instead of an excuse to do nothing.

You will be a source of inspiration.

FINAL THOUGHTS
# PRINCIPLE 4: SOULFUL

Modern persuasion doesn't have to be a soulless activity. On the contrary, the most uplifting and energizing forms of influence are those that resonate deep in our souls. When someone inspires us through sheer force of character, once-difficult things can seem easy, and ideas you thought were flat-out wrong can take on a new plausibility, and even a magnetism.

These sorts of experiences define soulful persuasion.

# The Last Word

"Persuasion" has become a bad word in today's culture, and my own industry, advertising, has been a contributor.

The notion of persuasion—and specifically advertising—as a nefarious activity dates back at least to social critic Vance Packard's 1957 book *The Hidden Persuaders*. In his landmark work, Packard uncovered the ways in which advertisers of that era used psychological research to turn consumers' unconscious desires against them. It was a stinging indictment of the industry, and in a lot of ways, we may have had it coming.

But *The Hidden Persuaders* isn't a book about persuasion. When psychology is used as a weapon to shape people to your will, it's not persuasion. It's manipulation. And manipulation is never defensible.

Persuasion is different. When you persuade someone, you

aren't tricking them into believing something, nor are you making them do something they wouldn't do if they saw things more clearly. Rather, you're inspiring them to make a specific choice of their own free will. You're leaving the decision up to them.

This crucial difference was made clear during the 2016 presidential election, when foreign actors abused social media to unfairly influence the race. Russian trolls were spreading misinformation and secretly preying on our unconscious biases to achieve a desired result. In other words, they were manipulating us.

By contrast, when candidates use social media to highlight certain facts, reveal parts of their personality, tell a specific story about the future of the country, or call on voters to do the right thing, they aren't cheating. They are playing the game fairly. And that's because they are persuading—not manipulating. You might not agree with them, but that's your choice. And that choice makes all the difference.

When someone inspires us to act on our own worst tendencies—on our sense of fear, hatred, or spite—that too is a form of persuasion, and a very powerful one at that. It's also possible to deploy persuasive techniques to get people to knowingly fight in unjust wars, or spend their money unwisely. Persuasion can be used for destructive purposes as well as good ones.

## Why Persuasion Matters

We can't forget that some of the most positive achievements in human history were made possible by acts of persuasion. Abraham Lincoln and Rosa Parks were both master persuaders who used their abilities to combat flagrant moral wrongs. Had they simply waited for people to change their minds independently, institutions like slavery and segregation would have remained the norm for far longer than they did. And the source of their influence was their own personal character.

A goal for this book is to bring the idea of persuasion into the twenty-first century by exploring an approach that gets its strength not from negativity and divisiveness but from the most laudable and positive aspects of our characters. At its best, persuasion is the most positive, productive, and ethical way of changing people's minds. It fully respects the idea that we are all free, equal individuals entitled to make our own decisions for our own reasons.

It's also an essential tool for addressing the most challenging problems we face right now. It's my deep belief that persuasion is the only resource we have for getting past our current moment of social strife, political polarization, toxic disagreement, and tribalism.

Yet most of our national conversation doesn't aim at persuasion. Whether in op-ed pieces or social media rants, our main modes of communication serve only to reinforce our existing beliefs and to cast those who disagree with us as inferior, backward, or even evil. Our public debates have become winner-take-all grudge matches. These social trends have turned us against one another and brought our national institutions to the brink of collapse.

This situation is simply unsustainable, especially in a country as diverse and individualistic as ours. If we are going to live well together, we'll need to be able to bring people over to our way of seeing things not by forcing them or shaming them or censoring their speech, but by convincing them. By persuading them.

## Character Makes a Comeback

There is a reason for optimism, because our current moment has also brought the importance of character to the fore. A number of social movements surrounding issues such as race, gender equality, and inclusiveness have started to raise expectations about the way we conduct ourselves in our private and public lives. Personal tendencies that were once ignored or at least tolerated—demeaning comments in the workplace, racism, bullying, and sexism—are being called out as unacceptable.

At the same time, unethical business practices are also getting the close scrutiny they have long deserved. Old ways of doing things—whether it's environmentally unsound manufacturing techniques, worker exploitation, or the careless and improper use of customer data—are chastised. The finished product or the bottom line is no longer the only thing that matters in the business world. The values that motivate a company and the way it conducts itself in the world—its character, in other words—is now a necessary component to long-term success.

As a result of this modern cultural shift, influence is more closely tied to one's character than ever before. It's no longer enough to endorse the right beliefs with your words. You need to embody those beliefs in your everyday life: the way you treat those around you, interact with your community and colleagues, and show respect for those from different cultures, backgrounds, and traditions. Our new norms are just beginning to take shape. And there is still plenty of progress to be made.

## Today Calls for Soulful Persuasion

Taken together, the forces shaping our culture right now have made the argument of soulful persuasion all the more urgent. We all need to be better soulful persuaders. And the path to effective persuasion starts by working on our own character. If you want to wield influence, you need to become the kind of person that people genuinely want to agree with—an original, generous, empathetic, and a soulful person. And following these practices helps to form habits.

> **HABIT 1:** *Being your own weird self* makes it difficult for others to see you as phony or manipulative, and allows them to recognize you as a unique individual.

> **HABIT 2:** *The power of storytelling* will help you to reframe contentious issues and offer your point of view in a way that resonates on a human level.

> **HABIT 3:** *Never be closing* and avoiding the "hard sell" will help demonstrate that you care about things other than your own immediate gain.

> **HABIT 4:** *Give yourself away* by seeking to give something away in every interaction. You'll be laying the groundwork for cooperation.

> **HABIT 5:** *The pull of positivity* counteracts the negative emotions that separate us.

> **HABIT 6:** *Just a little respect* can neutralize toxic "us versus them" thinking on the part of your audience.

**HABIT 7:** *It's not me, it's us* is the ability to see things from the perspective of others. Truly empathizing with someone else's point of view will enable you to meet your audience on their own terms and guide them to a new point of view.

**HABIT 8:** *Collaboration* will lead others to see you as a member of their team, making them far more likely to take your side now and in the future.

**HABIT 9:** *Finding common ground* involves learning to see people as basically similar. This will combat tribal tendencies in your own thinking and will help move others to do the same.

**HABIT 10:** *Skill-hunting* brings a high level of proficiency to everything that you do, lending you an innate authority that carries real influence.

**HABIT 11:** *Being a source of inspiration* will help others to move past their normal limitations and join you in your positive pursuits.

Crucially, these practices can't be adopted on a purely superficial level. In order for them to work as sources of persuasion, they need to be woven into your way of life so deeply that they become effortless, natural, and unconscious. They need to flow from your *soul*.

The four main principles and eleven habits will make you a more positive, happier person with more fulfilling experiences. These traits will also make you more influential in a wide range of situations both personally and professionally.

Strengthening our own character might not be the shortest route to influence, but it is the most effective one.

If you can see the value in becoming a more original, generous, empathetic, and soulful person, then consider yourself persuaded.

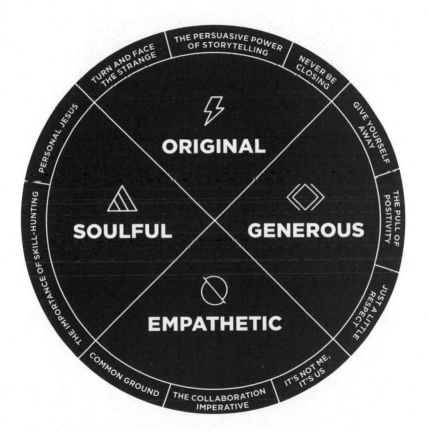

# Acknowledgments

*The Soulful Art of Persuasion* was developed from personal stories, role models, events, and deep research. I am grateful for the friends, family, and colleagues who helped me get this sucker across the finish line.

The team behind this book: Robert, Gretchen, Stephen, and Julia. And the publishing team at Random House/Currency and my star editor, Roger.

I would like to acknowledge the patience and smart advice from Karen and our two boys, Cole and Jett. The notes from my parents, Chuck and Sandy, and my sister, Stacey. And I want to thank my entire work family at Mekanism, and my original partners of thirteen years, Tommy, Ian, and Pete. And the guidance of Mike, Tom, and Brendan and the marketing chops of Meagan, Emma, and the support of Nina.

And I want to thank Tim Ferriss and Ryan Holiday for the endless inspiration of their work.

# Notes

## The Starting Point

1.  "Public Trust in Government: 1958–2017," Pew Research Center, December 14, 2017; Art Swift, "Democrats' Confidence in Mass Media Rises Sharply from 2016," Gallup, September 21, 2017.

2.  Casey Newton, "America Doesn't Trust Facebook," The Verge, October 27, 2017.

3.  Natalie Jackson and Grace Sparks, "A Poll Finds Most Americans Don't Trust Public Opinion Polls," *Huffington Post*, March 31, 2017.

4.  Frank Newport, "Congress Retains Low Honesty Rating," Gallup, December 3, 2012.

## Chapter 1

1.  Rob Sheffield, "Thanks, Starman: Why David Bowie Was the Greatest Rock Star Ever," *Rolling Stone*, January 11, 2016.

2. https://www.nytimes.com/2018/08/29/obituaries/lindsay -kemp-dead.html; https://www.theguardian.com/music /2016/jan/11/david-bowie-death-worldwide-tributes-death -work-of-art.

3. Christopher Mcquade, " 'I Loathed It': What David Bowie Learned from His Brief Spell in Adland," The Drum, January 11, 2016.

4. Angela Natividad, "Alligator, Space Invader: The Many Faces of David Bowie in Advertising," *Adweek*, January 11, 2016.

5. Aristotle, *Rhetoric*, trans. W. Rhys Roberts, I.2.

6. Leanne ten Brinke, Dayna Stimson, and Dana R. Carney, "Some Evidence for Unconscious Lie Detection," *Psychological Science* 25, no. 5 (2014).

7. ten Brinke, Stimson, and Carney, "Some Evidence."

8. Pamela Tom, "The Unconscious Mind Can Detect a Liar— Even When the Conscious Mind Fails," news release, Haas School of Business, University of California, Berkeley, March 27, 2014.

9. Paul C. Price and Eric R. Stone, "Intuitive Evaluation of Likelihood Judgment Producers: Evidence for a Confidence Heuristic," *Journal of Behavioral Decision Making* 17, no. 1 (2004): 39–57.

10. Lawrence Hosman, "Powerful and Powerless Speech Styles and Their Relationship to Perceived Dominance and Control," in *The Exercise of Power in Communication: Devices, Reception and Reaction*, edited by Rainer Schulze and Hanna Pishwa, 221–232 (New York: Palgrave Macmillan, 2015).

11. https://video.foxnews.com/v/5309865225001/#sp-show-clips.

12. Ezequias Rocha, "Sean McCabe," *Medium*, March 8, 2013.

## Chapter 2

1. Yuval Noah Harari, "Power and Imagination," http://www .ynharari.com/topic/power-and-imagination.

2. Daniel Smith et al., "Cooperation and the Evolution of Hunter-Gatherer Storytelling," *Nature Communications* 8 (2017): 1853.

3. Donald T. Phillips, *Lincoln on Leadership: Executive Strategies for Tough Times* (New York: Warner Books, 1992), 155.

4. Donald T. Phillips, *Lincoln Stories for Leaders: Influencing Others Through Storytelling* (Arlington, TX: Summit, 1997).

5. Doris Kearns Goodwin, *Team of Rivals: The Political Genius of Abraham Lincoln* (New York: Simon and Schuster, 2006), 713.

6. "Kiss—America's #1 Gold Record Award Winning Group of All Time," news release, Recording Industry Association of America, September 15, 2015.

7. Mikey Baird, "Top 10 Krazy Kiss Merchandise," *Hit the Floor Magazine*, May 14, 2014; Kiss action figures: http://www.kissarmywarehouse.com/action_figures_and_toys/; pocketknives: https://www.budk.com/KISS-Black-Folding-Knife-in-Collectible-Tin-14990; lip balm: http://www.kissarmywarehouse.com/the-spaceman-blister-pack-lip-balm/; bank checks: https://www.bradfordexchangechecks.com/products/1801119001-KISSand153-Personal-Check-Designs.html.

8. Keith Caulfield, "15 Surprising Artists Without a No. 1 Album," *Billboard*, August 11, 2014.

9. Melanie C. Green and Timothy C. Brock, "The Role of Transportation in the Persuasiveness of Public Narratives," *Journal of Personality and Social Psychology* 79, no. 5 (2000): 701–721.

10. Jennifer Aaker, "How to Use Stories to Win Over Others" (video), Lean In, https://leanin.org/education/harnessing-the-power-of-stories; Cody C. Delistraty, "The Psychological Comforts of Storytelling," *The Atlantic*, November 2, 2014.

11. Gus Cooney, Daniel T. Gilbert, and Timothy D. Wilson, "The Novelty Penalty: Why Do People Like Talking About New Experiences but Hearing About Old Ones?," *Psychological Science* 28, no. 3 (2017): 380–394.

12. Cooney, Gilbert, and Wilson, "The Novelty Penalty."

13. Cooney, Gilbert, and Wilson, "The Novelty Penalty."

14. Jonathan Haidt, *The Righteous Mind: Why Good People Are Divided by Politics and Religion* (New York: Vintage, 2013), 328.

## Chapter 3

1. Tom Peters, "The Brand Called You," *Fast Company*, August 31, 1997.

2. "Maximizing Your Personal Brand," course MKSB1-CE8500, School of Professional Studies, New York University; results of a search on "personal branding" at Coursera, https://www.coursera.org/courses?languages=en&query=personal%20branding.

3. Stacey Ross Cohen, "Personal Branding: A Must for the College-Bound, CEO and Everyone in Between," *Huffington Post*, updated December 6, 2017.

4. https://www.meaningful-brands.com/en.

5. Sivan Portal, Russell Abratt, and Michael Bendixen, "Building a Human Brand: Brand Anthropomorphism Unravelled," *Business Horizons* 61, no. 3 (2018): 367–374.

6. "'I Am a Brand,' Pathetic Man Says," *The Onion*, November 29, 2012.

7. Tristan Cooper, "McDonald's Let the Internet Create Their Own Burgers and Guess What Happened," Dorkly, July 20, 2016.

8. Connor Simpson, "The Internet Wants to Send Pitbull to an Alaskan Walmart," *Atlantic*, June 30, 2012; Sophie Schillaci, "Pitbull 'Exiled' to Alaska, Poses with Stuffed Bear at Walmart," *Hollywood Reporter*, July 30, 2012.

9. Todd Wasserman, "Congrats, Internet: Pitbull Is Going to Alaska," Mashable, July 17, 2012.

10. "Global Trust in Advertising: Winning Strategies for an Evolving Media Landscape," Nielsen, September 2015.

11. Joshua David Stein, "The Unfamous Man Who Made Everything Famous," *GQ*, October 5, 2016.

12. "How a Punch in the Face Sparked Shep Gordon's Incredible Hollywood Career," CBS News, November 12, 2016.

13. Melissa Gomez, "They Bought a Ghost Town for $1.4 Million. Now They Want to Revive It," *New York Times*, July 18, 2018.

14. Elaine Walster and Leon Festinger, "The Effectiveness of 'Overheard' Persuasive Communications," *Journal of Abnormal and Social Psychology* 65, no. 6 (1962): 395–402.

15. Brendan Gahan, "Limbic Resonance—The Science Behind the Success of YouTubers," December 2, 2014, http://brendangahan.com/limbic-resonance-science-behind-success-youtubers.

16. Rip Empson, "Twitter Buys TweetDeck for $40 Million," TechCrunch, May 23, 2011; Jason Kincaid, "Twitter Acquires Tweetie," TechCrunch, April 9, 2010.

17. "How to Make Ads That Even Savvy Customers Trust," Kellogg Insight, Kellogg School of Management, Northwestern University, April 13, 2017.

## Chapter 4

1. Robert B. Cialdini, *Influence: Science and Practice* (Boston: Pearson, 2009), 13.

2. "Principles of Persuasion" (video), https://www.influenceatwork.com/principles-of-persuasion.

3. Christian Smith, "What Makes Us Generous?," news release, University of Notre Dame, May 27, 2014.

4. Acts 20:35.

5. Richard Alan Krieger, ed., *Civilization's Quotations: Life's Ideal* (New York: Algora, 2007).

6. Jordan Michael Smith, "Want to Be Happy? Stop Being So Cheap!," *New Republic*, September 21, 2014; Elizabeth W. Dunn, Lara B. Aknin, and Michael I. Norton, "Prosocial Spending and Happiness: Using Money to Benefit Others Pays Off," *Current Directions in Psychological Science* 23, no. 1 (2014): 41–47; Ashley V. Whillans, Elizabeth W. Dunn, Gillian M. Sandstrom, Sally S. Dickerson, and Ken M. Madden, "Is Spending Money on Others Good for Your Heart?," *Health Psychology* 35, no. 6 (2016): 574–583; Elizabeth Renter, "What Generosity Does to Your Brain and Life Expectancy," *US News and World Report*, May 1, 2015.

7. Andrew W. Delton, Max M. Krasnow, Leda Cosmides, and John Tooby, "Evolution of Direct Reciprocity Under

Uncertainty Can Explain Human Generosity in One-Shot Encounters," *PNAS* 108, no. 32 (2011): 13335–13340.

8.  Geoffrey Forden, "False Alarms in the Nuclear Age," PBS, November 6, 2001; David Wright, "A Nuclear False Alarm That Looked Like the Real Thing," Union of Concerned Scientists, November 9, 2015.

9.  Christian B. Miller, "True Generosity Involves More than Just Giving," Aeon, May 4, 2018.

## Chapter 5

1.  Robert Mann, "How the 'Daisy' Ad Changed Everything About Political Advertising," *Smithsonian Magazine*, April 13, 2016.

2.  Daniel J. O'Keefe and Jakob D. Jensen, "Do Loss-Framed Persuasive Messages Engender Greater Message Processing than Do Gain-Framed Messages? A Meta-Analytic Review," *Communication Studies* 59, no. 1 (2008): 51–67.

3.  Stanley Schachter and Jerome E. Singer, "Cognitive, Social, and Physiological Determinants of Emotional State," *Psychological Review* 69, no. 5 (1962): 379–399.

4.  John B. Judis, "Nobody Likes Mitt," *New Republic*, September 13, 2012.

5.  Lynda Mae, Donal E. Carlston, and John J. Skowronski, "Spontaneous Trait Transference to Familiar Communications: Is a Little Knowledge a Dangerous Thing?," *Journal of Personality and Social Psychology* 77, no. 2 (1999): 233–246.

6.  Alison Wood Brooks, "Get Excited: Reappraising Pre-Performance Anxiety as Excitement," *Journal of Experimental Psychology* 143, no. 3 (2014): 1144–1158.

## Chapter 6

1.  Christine Porath, "Half of Employees Don't Feel Respected by Their Bosses," *Harvard Business Review*, November 19, 2014.

2.  "The Rescue of Deputy Moon: Hero Inmates Save Lone Guard as He's Choked by Prisoner in Violent Attack," *Daily Mail*, November 6, 2009.

3. "Inmates Recount How They Saved Deputy from Attack," *Tampa Bay Tribune*, November 5, 2009.

4. Quoted in Edward Alexander Westermarck, *Christianity and Morals* (1931; New York: Routledge, 2013).

5. "The Sentences of Sextus," trans. Frederik Wisse, Nag Hammadi Library, Gnostic Society Library, http://www.gnosis.org/naghamm/sent.html.

6. Quoted in Westermarck, *Christianity and Morals*, 71.

7. Leviticus 19:18.

8. E. M. Bowden, comp., *The Essence of Buddhism* (Girard, KS: Haldeman-Julius, 1922).

9. Gurcharan Das, "Draupadi's Question: Lessons for Public and Corporate Governance," in *Textuality and Inter-Textuality in the Mahabharata*, edited by Pradeep Trikha (New Delhi: Sarup and Sons, 2006), 121.

10. Jeffrey Wattles, *The Golden Rule* (New York: Oxford University Press, 1996), 192.

11. Porath, "Half of Employees Don't Feel Respected by Their Bosses."

12. William Safire, "On Language: The Elision Fields," *New York Times Magazine*, August 13, 1989.

13. Mariek Vanden Abeele, Marjolijn Antheunis, and Alexander Schouten, "The Effect of Mobile Messaging During a Conversation on Impression Formation and Interaction Quality," *Computers in Human Behavior* 62 (2016): 562–569.

14. Varoth Chotpitayasunondh and Karen M. Douglas, "The Effects of 'Phubbing' on Social Interaction," *Journal of Applied Social Psychology* (online), January 24, 2018, DOI: 10.1111/jasp.12506.

15. Suzanne Wu, "Was It Smart to Use Your Phone at That Meeting?," news release, University of Southern California, October 24, 2013.

16. Andrea Park, "Disney Drops Director James Gunn from 'Guardians of the Galaxy' over Offensive Tweets," CBS News, July 20, 2018.

17. Alison Mitchell, "Impeachment: The Overview—Clinton Impeached; He Faces a Senate Trial, 2d in History; Vows to Do Job till Term's 'Last Hour,'" *New York Times*, December 20, 1998.

18. "Anthony Weiner Scandal: A Timeline," CNN, updated August 30, 2016.

## Chapter 7

1. Shanto Iyengar, Gaurav Sood, and Yphtach Lelkes, "Affect, Not Ideology: A Social Identity Perspective on Polarization," *Public Opinion Quarterly* 76, no. 3 (2012): 405–431.

2. Lynn Vavreck, "A Measure of Identity: Are You Married to Your Party?," *New York Times*, January 31, 2017.

3. "Trayvon Martin Shooting Fast Facts," CNN, updated June 5, 2013.

4. Amy Davidson Sorkin, "'If I Had a Son, He'd Look Like Trayvon,'" *New Yorker*, March 23, 2012.

5. Sorkin, "'If I Had a Son.'"

6. Bill Demain, "Ten Days in a Madhouse: The Woman Who Got Herself Committed," Mental Floss, May 2, 2011.

7. "Empathy Is Key to Political Persuasion, Shows New Research," news release, Rotman School of Management, University of Toronto, November 11, 2015.

8. "Empathy Is Key to Political Persuasion."

9. "Empathy Is Key to Political Persuasion."

10. Cal Fussman, "5 Tips to Develop Your Own Big Questions," https://convertkit.s3.amazonaws.com/landing_pages/incentives/000/361/656/original/CalFussman_5Tips.pdf?1533062919.

11. Richard Feldman, "Charity, Principle Of," *Routledge Encyclopedia of Philosophy* (online).

## Chapter 8

1. Henri Tajfel, "Social Psychology of Intergroup Relations," *Annual Review of Psychology* 33 (1982): 23.

2. James H. Stark and Douglas N. Frenkel, "Changing Minds: The Work of Mediators and Empirical Studies of Persuasion," *Ohio State Journal on Dispute Resolution* 28 (2013): 263–356.

3. E. Aronson, "The Power of Self-Persuasion," *American Psychologist* 54, no. 11 (1999): 875–884.

4. https://psycnet.apa.org/record/1970-10278-001.

5. Pew Research Center, "Changing Attitudes on Gay Marriage," June 26, 2017.

6. "In-Depth Topics A to Z: Marriage," Gallup, https://news.gallup.com/poll/117328/marriage.aspx.

7. Adam Liptak, "Supreme Court Ruling Makes Same-Sex Marriage a Right Nationwide," *New York Times*, June 27, 2015.

8. Alex Tribou and Keith Collins, "This Is How Fast America Changes Its Mind," Bloomberg, updated June 26, 2015.

9. Pew Research Center, "Where the Public Stands on Religious Liberty vs. Nondiscrimination," September 28, 2016.

10. Daniel Cox and Harmeet Kamboj, "How Social Contact with LGBT People Impacts Attitudes on Policy," Public Religion Research Institute, June 7, 2017.

11. Joe Otterson, "TV Ratings: Super Bowl LII Slips 7% from 2017 to 103.4 Million Viewers," *Variety*, February 5, 2018.

12. Bradley Johnson, "Big Game Punting: Super Bowl Scores $5.4 Billion in Ad Spending over 52 Years," *Ad Age*, January 11, 2018.

13. Tanza Loudenback, "Middle-Class Americans Made More Money Last Year than Ever Before," *Business Insider*, September 12, 2017.

14. Ben Franklin, *The Autobiography of Ben Franklin*, ed. Frank Woodward Pine (New York: Henry Holt, 1916), Chapter X.

15. Yu Niiya, "Does a Favor Request Increase Liking Toward the Requester?," *Journal of Social Psychology* 156, no. 2 (2016): 211–221.

16. Shana Lebowitz, "A Psychologist Says a Small Tweak to the Questions You Ask Your Boss Can Make Them Think Better of You," *Business Insider*, September 15, 2016.

17. Wendy Liu and David Gal, "Bringing Us Together or Driving Us Apart: The Effect of Soliciting Consumer Input on Consumers' Propensity to Transact with an Organization," *Journal of Consumer Research* 38, no. 2 (2010): 242.

18. "All the Great Mad Men Era Volkswagen Ads," BuzzFeed, September 1, 2013.

## Chapter 9

1. National Human Genome Research Institute, "Frequently Asked Questions About Genetic and Genomic Science," https://www.genome.gov/19016904/faq-about-genetic-and -genomic-science.

2. Sha Be Allah, "Today in Hip Hop History: Kool Herc's Party at 1520 Sedgwick Avenue 45 Years Ago Marks the Foundation of the Culture Known as Hip Hop," *The Source*, August 11, 2018.

3. Amos Barshad, "Rude Boys," *New York Magazine*, April 24, 2011.

4. Sha Be Allah, "Today in Hip-Hop History: Run-DMC Drops 'Walk This Way' Featuring Aerosmith 31 Years Ago," *The Source*, July 4, 2017.

5. Samir Meghelli, "Hip-Hop à la Française," *New York Times*, updated October 15, 2013; Johann Voigt, "From Russia with Flow: How Rap Became Russia's Most Important Genre," *Noisey*, March 22, 2018; Victoria Namkung, "Seoul's Bumping B-Boy Scene," *New York Times*, December 16, 2017; P. Khalil Saucier and Kumarini Silva, "Keeping It Real in the Global South: Hip-Hop Comes to Sri Lanka," *Critical Sociology* 40, no. 2 (2014): 295–300.

6. Jay-Z, *Decoded* (New York: Spiegel & Grau, 2010).

7. Nick Joyce and Jake Harwood, "Context and Identification in Persuasive Mass Communication," *Journal of Media Psychology* 26, no. 1 (2014): 50–57.

8. Naina Bajekal, "Silent Night: The Story of the World War I Christmas Truce of 1914," *Time*, December 24, 2014.

9. David Brown, "Remembering a Victory for Human Kindness," *Washington Post*, December 25, 2004.

10. Nadège Mougel, "World War I Casualties," trans. Julie Gratz, Centre Européen Robert Schuman, 2011.

11. Peter Kaufman, "The Similarities Project," *Everyday Sociology Blog*, December 5, 2011, http://www.everydaysociologyblog .com/2011/12/the-similarities-project.html.

12. Kaufman, "The Similarities Project."

13. Kaufman, "The Similarities Project."

14. Dan Primack, "Unilever Buys Dollar Shave Club for $1 Billion," *Fortune*, July 19, 2016.

## Chapter 10

1. Anita Elberse and Jeroen Verleun, "The Economic Value of Celebrity Endorsements," *Journal of Advertising Research*, June 2012, 149–165.

2. Kenneth T. Walsh, "Tom Hanks Is Most Trusted American, Obama Far Behind," *US News and World Report*, May 9, 2013.

3. Tim Ferriss, "How to Breakdance 101: Unleash Your Inner B-Boy," October 25, 2009, https://tim.blog/2009/10/25/how -to-breakdance-101; Tim Ferriss, "How to Lose 30 Pounds in 24 Hours: The Definitive Guide to Cutting Weight," January 18, 2008, https://tim.blog/tag/dehydration.

4. "Hack," Techopedia, https://www.techopedia.com/definition /27859/hack-development.

5. Nat Eliason, "No More 'Struggle Porn,'" Medium, October 18, 2018.

6. "Company Info," Patagonia, https://www.patagonia.com /company-info.html.

7. Jon Porter, "The New MacBook Air and Mac Mini Are Made of 100 Percent Recycled Aluminum," The Verge, October 30, 2018; Nick Statt, "Apple Says It's Now Powered by 100 Percent Renewable Energy Worldwide," The Verge, April 9, 2018.

8. Walmart, "2018 Global Responsibility Report."

9. K. Anders Ericsson, Michael J. Prietula, and Edward T. Cokely, "The Making of an Expert," *Harvard Business Review*, July–August 2007.

10.   Mike Berardino, "Mike Tyson Explains One of His Most Famous Quotes," *Sun-Sentinel*, November 9, 2012.

## Chapter 11

1.    Andrew Wolfson, "Muhammad Ali Lost Everything in Opposing the Vietnam War. But in 1968, He Triumphed," *USA Today*, February 19, 2018.

2.    Jim Weeks, "How Muhammad Ali Stunned the World at the Rumble in the Jungle," Vice Sports, June 29, 2017.

3.    Stephanie Merry, "Her Shocking Murder Became the Stuff of Legend. But Everyone Got the Story Wrong," *Washington Post*, June 29, 2016.

4.    John M. Darley and Bibb Latané, "Bystander Intervention in Emergencies: Diffusion of Responsibility," *Journal of Personality and Social Psychology* 8 (1968): 377–383.

5.    Darley and Latané, "Bystander Intervention in Emergencies."

6.    Jennifer M. Wood, "15 Inspiring Quotes from Rosa Parks," Mental Floss, February 4, 2018.

7.    "63 Years Ago, Rosa Parks Stood Up for Civil Rights by Sitting Down," CNN, December 1, 2018.

8.    U.S. Green Building Council, "Up-to-Date, Official Statistics About USGBC Programs," October 2017, https://www.usgbc .org/articles/usgbc-statistics.

9.    U.S. Green Building Council, "Benefits of Green Building," https://www.usgbc.org/articles/green-building-facts.

10.   U.S. Green Building Council, "Benefits of Green Building."

11.   Mairi Beautyman, "Write Your Own Eulogy, Says Father of LEED David Gottfried to a Crowd in Las Vegas," TreeHugger, June 17, 2008.

12.   Better Make Room, https://www.bettermakeroom.org; Stand Stronger, https://committocitizenship.org; The United State of Women, https://www.theunitedstateofwomen.org.

13.   "About Dr. King Overview," The King Center, http://www .thekingcenter.org/about-dr-king; Emily Wax, "Martin Lu-

ther King's Nonviolent Civil Rights Efforts Still Inspire Across Globe," *Washington Post*, July 27, 2011.

14. "About StreetVet," https://www.streetvet.co.uk/about.

15. "About T|H Models," http://www.tihmodels.com/about.

16. Penelope Lockwood and Ziva Kunda, "Superstars and Me: Predicting the Impact of Role Models on the Self," *Journal of Personality and Social Psychology* 73, no. 1 (1997): 91–103.

# Index

# About the Author

Jason Harris is the CEO of the award-winning creative agency Mekanism and the cofounder of the Creative Alliance. Harris works closely with brands through a blend of soul and science to create provocative campaigns that engage audiences. Iconic brands include Peloton, Ben & Jerry's, Miller Coors, HBO, and the United Nations. Under his leadership, Mekanism was named to *Ad Age*'s Agency A-list and twice to their Best Places to Work, and to *Creativity*'s Creativity 50. Harris has been named in the Top 10 Most Influential Social Impact Leaders, as well as the 4A's list of "100 People Who Make Advertising Great." His methods are studied at Harvard Business School.